1 25

Martin Meyer's
MONEYBOOK

By the Same Author

Don't Bank on It!
(with J. M. McDaniel, Jr.)

Credit-Cardsmanship

Martin Meyer's
MONEYBOOK

Yes, You CAN Earn 10.4 to 23.5% on Your Savings —Federally Insured

Plus 51 More MONEY KEYS To Build Your Estate from Scratch—Legally

by MARTIN J. MEYER

with a foreword by Dr. Joseph M. McDaniel, Jr.

Published by
BOOKS FOR BETTER LIVING
Trade distribution by
SIMON AND SCHUSTER

Published in New York City by
Books for Better Living Division
Curtis Books, Inc.
and simultaneously in Toronto, Canada, by
Curtis Distributing, Ltd.
Subsidiaries of Cadence Industries Corporation
641 Lexington Avenue, New York, New York 10022

Book trade distribution by
Simon and Schuster
Rockefeller Center, 630 Fifth Avenue
New York, N.Y. 10020

Library of Congress Catalog Card Number 79-92845
International Standard Book Number 0-502-00000-7

PRINTED AND BOUND IN THE U.S.A.

To Mac and Shelly

Contents

The lines in italics designate MONEY KEYS

BONUS

Foreword

You will derive great pleasure from reading this book. Far more important, you will find that it brings you keys, very valuable keys, to unlock doors that lead to a better, fuller, and richer life.

These keys have not been fashioned by professional economists; seldom do those "experts" agree on a specific solution to a specific problem, as do other scientists. For example, if I were to go to three doctors and say to each, "On my right side, I have a pain above my leg. It's over toward the middle of my stomach," all three doctors would agree, after an examination, that I was suffering from appendicitis, and they would know what to do. Yet the most eminent practitioners in the field of economics seemingly cannot agree on what the basic causes of our financial maladies are, much less what steps should be taken to correct them.

When you have a professed science in which the "professionals" disagree as sharply as they do in economics, great opportunities are opened to the gifted and experienced nonprofessional man of action. He can move in and bring his hard-earned insights and intuition to bear on the vital problems and the needed solutions. As a matter of fact, some major contributions to the study of economics have been made by individuals who followed other vocations with great success and looked upon economics as an avocation. Some of the greatest names in the field, such as Adam Smith, Thomas Malthus, and David Ricardo, fall snugly into this category. To this illustrious roster

11

the name of Martin Meyer could well be added.

Martin Meyer has brought fresh and exciting insights to the general field of economics. He has illuminated areas that professionals have failed to light up because they have become the captives of the sanctified knowledge of the past. Martin Meyer, by eliminating the esoteric, makes the mystery of the science of economics disappear. His down-to-earth view of what makes the world turn financially brings reality out of obscurantism. He understands that each of us strives to make a living, and he shows us how to get the most from the living we make.

Even if the professional economist were to offer suggestions to help you live better, unfortunately you would not be able to penetrate his specialized language. The professional economist seems to find a special satisfaction in the use of a complex jargon far beyond the comprehension of the man in the street. Martin Meyer takes this complicated verbiage and turns it into simple language—accurately. He makes his contributions to your financial well-being understandable and therefore useful.

Get acquainted with Martin Meyer's MONEY KEYS to better living by reading the introductory chapters with care. After that, it is not necessary to look upon the chapters that follow as a rigid menu in which you must start with soup and follow through to dessert. Think of this book as a smorgasbord, in which you look over the broad selection and pick the delights that specially attract you.

This volume will be followed by others, but to bridge the period between the publication of this book and the appearance of the next, Martin Meyer will issue other publications at regular intervals, offering you additional MONEY KEYS that you will find highly useful. I, for one, am looking forward to his forthcoming efforts. I am confident that they will continue to provide exceptional information that you cannot find elsewhere

—information that will help you live far better on your income than you ever thought possible.

Dr. Joseph M. McDaniel, Jr.

Dr. McDaniel is former Dean, School of Business, Northwestern University; Secretary of the Ford Foundation, retired; Member, Board of Directors, United Brands; Trustee, Johns Hopkins University.

Build your estate
with this tool

A tool is not a toy to be played with. It should be used for the purpose for which it was made. Like a hammer, screw-driver, or saw, this book is a tool. It's a tool that was made with the express purpose of helping you become rich. It's your tool to use.

This tool, this book, is designed to help you achieve your goal of riches through three guidelines.

The first tells you how to develop a special, enjoyable way of life which enables you to *find* the money with which you can start building and continue to build your estate.

The second shows you how to keep your estate constantly increasing in value through what I call MONEY KEYS.

The third upsets some of your prejudices, giving you new insights so that you, as an individual, can make this place a better place, not only for yourself but for all. Don't be the one who says, "I never read because reading makes me think, and thinking upsets my prejudices."

Some of the specific plans in each of the three guidelines will be attractive to you, and you will follow them eagerly. Some may not be to your liking. Those you may very well ignore. But the *more* specific plans you follow, the surer you'll be that you'll become richer.

Most of the guidelines will make more and more money for you. If you waste that money, you will never be any richer than you are today. But add that money to your estate, and you will not only be richer in dollars but also in the sense of having achieved a goal that is unattainable to the vast majority of people.

Use this tool. Use it well. Enjoy its use and the product of its use—riches.

Today is your Fourth of July

Yes, today is your Fourth of July. Today is your own personal Independence Day, the day on which you will start your climb toward wealth, security, peace of mind, self-fulfillment, a better life for yourself, and a better and safer life for your children. These United States started with a Declaration of Independence; to gain our independence, first we declared it, then we worked successfully to make a new and wonderful way of life for ourselves. Similarly, after *your* Declaration of Independence today, you're going to change some of your modes of living and some of your ways of thinking. You're going to go through a personal revolution to achieve individual goals as worthy as the national goals of our American Revolution.

Whoever dreamed on July 4, 1776, that from those small, weak colonies would grow the most powerful, most influential nation on earth—merely from the simple act of declaring independence and then going forward. You can grow just as surely by declaring your independence now and following the guidelines and the MONEY KEYS in this book to achieve and secure that independence. You'll create for yourself, and for your children and your childrens' children, the power and the glory and the grandeur that the Declaration of Independence created for our country.

Get rich quick? No!
Get rich slow

Only the very few get rich quick. You can get rich quick too if you bear or sire sextuplets, if you get your own talk show, or if you were born 7 feet 10 inches tall and have a bent for basketball.

Barring such lucky breaks, however, you too can become rich, but more slowly.

The formulas are simple, the medicine is sweet, and the benefits are permanent.

Even if you are now flat broke, in debt over your head— if you can earn just the average American living, you can start on the road to riches today. YES, YOU *CAN!*

And along with your riches you will acquire a sense of security, an enviable reputation, self-esteem, a better and fuller life. You will be secure in the knowledge that you have been in the right, as God and good common sense have given you to see the right.

The attitude that can
make you rich
—starting from scratch

I have built a sizable estate. I started building that estate when my family was on welfare; when my father, who had been sick for many years, was flat on his back unable to move; and when we didn't have enough to eat. I didn't have a pair of shoes— only a pair of sneakers into which I stuffed cardboard to cover the holes in the bottom. I was twelve years old.

I would estimate that today my estate is probably larger than the estates of 95% of the people in this country. But I'm no Horatio Alger. I never made a killing in the stock market. I never made it big in any way. And for almost 20 years, the tremendous cost of caring for my aged and infirm mother was deducted from my earnings. My income was never much higher than the salary of the average college-trained man or woman in the United States. Yet the income from my estate is now large enough to keep my family and me living decently for the rest of my life—even if I should never be able to work again.

In the past nine years in particular, my average annual earnings were probably less than half of what the garbage man makes. But my estate is large enough that, with the income from it, I've been able to live for these past nine years in my own home and almost pay off my mortgage. Just the taxes on my home were $4,400 this year.

The income from my estate makes this good life possible. Yet so many people I know who have had far greater average incomes per year than mine have no estates. In my entire lifetime I haven't earned what people like Joe Louis or Mickey Rooney earned in one year—yet these people went broke and I built a substantial estate. What was the difference between them and me? Was I more intelligent? Was I luckier? Shrewder? Absolutely not! I'm very much like everybody else. Looking back over my life, trying to figure out how I built my substantial estate from a modest income, I realize that it all began with a special *attitude*. You can be sure it's *not* the attitude of those people who never built estates, even though their incomes were greater than mine. What's so special about my attitude? I believe I can give you an idea by telling you a story.

I think back to the time when my family was extremely poor. I was going to high school. I was very young, just twelve. Most kids my age were still in grammar school. My high school was almost 3¾ miles away from my home. In those days the subway and trolley car fares were only 5 cents, but there were times when I didn't have the dime to make the round trip. Somehow my mother managed to scrape up the money if the weather was bad; but if it was a nice spring day, or a nice autumn day, 5 cents could be better used for food and I ended up with only a nickel for carefare. I would take the subway to school in the morning, and after school I would walk home. Those were the days when people didn't mind walking. We weren't used to riding every bit of the way. I found that this 3¾-mile walk was enjoyable. I got to know more of the city. Sometimes a classmate who lived along the way would walk with me even though he had the money to take the subway.

There were times when I *had* the dime for carfare, but I preferred to walk home and save the nickel. Why did I want to save the nickel? I was very fond of Hershey's nickel chocolate bars, which I seldom had. A piece of candy was just not on my menu; there was no money for it. But—and here's where that special attitude started to develop—I did *not* use the nickel to buy a Hershey bar. That was because all the chain drug and sundry stores at that time sold the nickel candies three for a dime; so I disciplined myself and I didn't buy the candy until I had saved up a dime. Then I bought three Hershey bars. There were other candies I liked, and sometimes I bought one Hershey bar and a package of Planters Peanuts and a Mason Mint—all three for a dime. I didn't permit myself to become a glutton and eat all the candies at one time as many kids would have done. I ate the Hershey bar and saved the other two candies until the next time I felt that I was entitled to a treat. Then, instead of having to buy candy, I already had it. When I finally got around to eating the third package, I felt I was getting it free. In this way I reduced the cost of my candy eating by 33.33%.

So that was the beginning of the development of my attitude. It can be summed up this way:

I deferred my pleasures for a short while and saved my money. Then I used my savings to buy more for less. I enjoyed the things I wanted—at a discount!

Let me go on with my school-days story, and I'll show you how my special attitude continued to take shape.

I took particular note of the kind of candy bars that were most popular among the boys that I knew. They were Nestle bars, Hershey bars, Mr. Goodbar, and Milky Ways—candies of that type. The school lunchroom didn't carry these candies, and the boys would have to leave the school and go to a candy store to get them. I got the idea that I could easily sell these candies to the boys in the school for a nickel each, because that would save the boys the trouble of having to leave the school to buy the candies. But there would be no profit for me if I bought the candies for a nickel and sold them for a nickel, so I walked a couple of blocks to get them three for a dime.

I raised the money to buy the candies by saving on my subway fare. When I was given a dime, I walked home and saved the nickel, just as I did when I bought the candy bars three for a dime for myself. Only I didn't save up just a dime. I waited until I had saved 30 cents, and I plunged in a big investment. For 30 cents, at three for a dime, I got nine bars of candy instead of the six bars I would have gotten at a nickel each. In one day, I sold those nine bars of candy for a nickel apiece to the kids in the school during lunchtime or right before lunch. I started with 30 cents, and soon I had 45 cents!

The next day I bought more candy bars. Before I knew it, I had my briefcase half full of candy bars. I was in business.

Then I realized if the stores at which I was buying the candy bars were selling these candies three for a dime, somebody must be selling the candies to the stores cheaper. So I looked around. I found a place about eight blocks away from the high school that sold the candies wholesale to peddlers. I was able to buy a box of 24 bars for 72 cents. I had the 72 cents because I was saving every cent I made from my little candy business. Now here's the arithmetic:

Three for a dime comes to 3⅓ cents apiece. A box of 24 bars for 72 cents comes to 3 cents a bar. So instead of making 1⅔ cents on each bar I sold for a nickel, I made 2 cents. A small difference? Well, on every three bars I sold I now made 6 cents instead of a nickel. And with every 15 bars I sold, I made another nickel. To me, that wasn't a small difference.

Or look at it this way: Three for a dime amounted to a 33.33% discount from the 5-cent retail price. A cost of 3 cents each amounted to a 40% discount.

I went back to the wholesaler several times to buy boxes of candy bars at 72 cents apiece. One day when I was about to make a purchase, I saw a peddler who was buying a couple of boxes end up paying only 60 cents a box. I complained to the wholesaler. He told me if someone walked in for just one box of candy, the charge was 72 cents, but for a regular customer the price was 60 cents. "Since you've become a regular customer," the wholesaler said, "you get them for 60 cents." This wholesale discount came to 50% off! I paid 60 cents and sold those bars of candy for $1.20. I was able to double my money every few days.

I was earning something like 25 cents a day. I was able to pay my own carfare; I was able to pay for my lunches; and I was able to remove this financial load from my parents, who were suffering terribly. And out of this little business of mine came something which was very important to a boy: I was able to have an occasional dessert of a piece of candy. Doesn't every young boy want that? I remember once I really splurged and had a package of Planters Peanuts and a Mason Mint both in one day *at the same time!* They seemed even tastier because my cost was only a nickel for the *two* of them.

Because of the money I earned, I was able to stop bringing dry, tasteless sandwiches from home; I was able to go down to the restaurant across the street from the school, get a big hamburger, with all the side dishes you could get for nothing with a hamburger in those days, and complete my meal with a soft drink—all for the big sum of one dime. But remember, if I hadn't saved and *got the most from my savings*, I wouldn't have had that dime, and I wouldn't have been able to enjoy myself.

So my attitude had developed along these lines:

I didn't save just to get the things I wanted at the lowest prices. I got the most from my savings first. And I used the money I earned on my savings to buy the things that made me happy.

Later in life I realized that I had then completed the development of my attitude—an attitude that has guided me ever since. It's an attitude that can make you rich. This is it:

Save.
Get the most from your savings.
Use the money you make on your savings to buy the things you want—at the lowest prices.

By applying this attitude—while you're saving and watching your savings multiply—you're building a nest egg, an estate. So you're not only living better for less but also ensuring against any financial problems in the future. You're taking care of all the emergencies that may arise. You're providing security for yourself and for your loved ones.

Money Key No. 1

The master key to riches:
found money

Each individual has his own idea of what "rich" means. It could mean living for a year without working, having the money for an around-the-world cruise, or being able to reach any of a number of other desirable goals. To accomplish any of these you must have an estate or a nest egg—unless you have a favorite rich uncle who is expected to will you a fortune.

Do you want to be rich? If by "rich" you mean having that nest egg *and* watching that nest egg grow, then, YES, YOU *CAN* be rich. All you have to do is follow the MONEY KEYS and the other guidelines in this book. Then, even if you're on welfare now, you'll have to become rich eventually.

What you start off with is what I call THE MASTER KEY. It's the most important *Key* to riches. It's a new habit which you can easily acquire. It's a habit which develops into a whole new way of living—a life-style that sets you apart from the crowd. It's the *found money* habit.

With found money, you can start your nest egg. If you've already started your nest egg, found money will help you build it.

How shall I describe found money?

I guess I can start by telling you about the person whose automobile is a couple of years old and who feels he's out of style. He chafes at the bit looking for some excuse to get a new car. "My car isn't worth fixing anymore," he tells himself. "I'm better off getting a new car." So instead of putting $300 into repairs on his old car, he goes out and spends $4,000 for a new car.

Did he *have* to have a *new* car? With only $300 worth of repairs, his old car could have gotten him around just as well as his new car, which cost him $4,000.

"But I needed a new car for prestige," this person will say to defend his purchase. And he'll add, "There's just no answer to *that*."

But there *is* an answer.

I've had the same car for over 15 years, and that car now has more prestige than most newer cars. I own a Mercedes Benz, bought in 1955. Because I've kept it for so long, the cost per year is more like the cost of owning a motorcycle. I have all the prestige I want. And I have something more—something far, far more important: I have the satisfaction of knowing I didn't spend my hard-earned money year after year for a new car that I didn't really need.

The difference between the cost of repairs and the cost of a new car—*that's* found money.

Let me give you another example:

A lot of people fool themselves into believing they need something just because it's stylish. Every time some new style comes out, they rush out to buy it. If pants are pegged a little more or belled a little more, or if stores are showing 1/4-inch-longer shirt collars—what happens? Into dead storage or into the garbage goes all the good clothing. What a waste of money! The people who do this argue: "We make a more impressive appearance when we wear the new styles, and we're respected more."

Really?

The people who are really respected in this world, the

people who are looked up to, couldn't care less what they wear. They don't dress in style. It's the little guy—"little" in the sense that he's done nothing to really gain respect and admiration—who changes his wardrobe with every change of fad. In no way does he really improve the way people regard him. He's really fooling himself if he thinks he's a bigger or better man for being in the height of fashion. He could wear his old clothes with the same amount of respect as his new ones if people knew his money was going into a bank account instead of into a frivolous, unnecessary new suit. As a matter of fact, he'd be treated with more respect; everybody would regard him as a far bigger man and a far better man.

The amount of money saved by *not* listening to the dictates of fashion—*that's* found money.

One more example:

There are some women who convince themselves that they'll look like twenty-year-olds again if they smear gook on their faces. A multibillion dollar industry has been built up taking advantage of women like these. Face creams and all sorts of cosmetics are supposed to make these women younger looking, better looking, more attractive—but all these preparations are basically frauds. What makes the use of them so much more tragic is that most women look best—youngest and prettiest—when they use just plain soap and water, eat right, and get enough sleep and exercise. And all *that* costs very little.

So the woman who resists the high-priced advertising campaigns for this hair spray and that lipstick and this perfume and that face cream ends up with extra money in her purse, and *that's* found money.

You see, there are two ways to get the things you want in life: the "keeping up with the Joneses" way and the "found money" way. When you keep up with the Joneses, more often than not you *don't* get the good things you want, and you pay a terrible price for what you get. Do you remember the Bible story of Jonah? Jonah was supposed to be a bad-luck guy, which was why he was thrown overboard—and that's how he got swallowed by the whale. A Jonah is a bad-luck person. When a person tries to keep up with the Joneses, he's really trying to keep up with the Jonahs.

But if you get into the habit of resisting the phony life-style—and all the advertising lures that try to trap you into that life-style—and you get what you want *sensibly*, then you'll *find* money in your pocket. *That's* the found money habit.

So whenever you have a choice, no matter what your walk of life, between the phony life-style—keeping up with the Jonahs—and the sensible life-style—the found money habit—choose the life-style that's sure to pay off. Once you get into the found money habit, you'll find the money to start your estate and build your estate *right in your own income*. You'll find the money you *were* throwing away in your own pocket instead. From your pocket it will go into the bank or into other safe investments; and it will multiply when you follow the MONEY KEYS.

So resist temptation to spend every cent in your jeans. Just think: Each time you save just $100 of found money, that $100 provides you with $6 to $15 a year or more for every year of your life. And you still have the original $100. And with more and more found money, your estate will grow bigger and bigger.

When you're rich, remember what made it possible, THE MASTER KEY to riches: found money.

Take advantage of advantages

Bankers seldom make mistakes. When they make a rule that can work to your advantage, don't assume the bankers don't know about it.

When you use the MONEY KEYS, you simply take advantage of advantages offered you by the banks and financial organizations. When you do this, it means more business for the banks and financial organizations in the long run. That's why the advantages were put there in the first place. Take advantage of the advantages.

Don't smash the banks' windows— share their profits

I could tell you of all the things that are wrong in our society. All the ways you are being cheated. All the ways that you don't get a fair shake. All the ways that the establishment supposedly operates against you. All the ways that you are exploited. All the ways you are taken advantage of. All the ways you are fooled, tricked, or robbed. But what purpose would that serve? It would get you angry. It would get you upset. It would make you unhappy.

To what extent would that change things? You might possibly join movements that look to create change. You might even become a revolutionary. You might be incited to riot, to burn, pillage, wreck, or destroy. And what would that do for you? It might be an outlet for your anger and frustration, but that would simply put you in the same class as the hippies, yippies, zippies, and their fellow travelers who want to tear down our society and build nothing in return. History has shown us that violent reactions to circumstances seldom produce good for anybody. Everybody loses.

No, just telling you what's wrong is no way of making things better. Yet isn't that what almost every "expert" tells you? Elizabeth M. Fowler writes in *The New York Times* that "the shelves of libraries are overflowing with diagnoses of what's wrong with today's society and pitifully barren of work-

30

able and concrete suggestions on how to rectify matters." But this book takes up where all those other books leave off.

I recognize that we are all faced with many unfair situations and that change is slow in coming. But through this book you will learn that these very situations can be turned to your advantage. By *you*. By *yourself*. *Without* joining any groups. *Without* taking part in any demonstrations. *Without* relying on do-gooders to help you. YES, YOU *CAN* do it. You can turn the very strengths of the "establishment" that seem to operate against you to your advantage. You'll find that what you regarded as unfair practices are really advantages built into our system—for your individual profit if you know how to take advantage of the advantages. It was a very small David with a very small pebble that managed to slay the giant Goliath. You, as a small individual, armed with the knowledge of the advantages of our system as explained in the MONEY KEYS, can easily be the victor.

Let me emphasize this: The Ralph Naders, the Bess Myersons, and all the hundreds of consumer activists across the country have done a good job of alerting us to all the things that are wrong. They have done a good job of dissatisfying each of us with what goes on. But it may take decades, it may take centuries, before any major percentage of these wrongs are righted through the efforts of the consumer activists. Yet remembering how many of these so-called wrongs really are advantages to you—once you see them for what they are—it need take *only days* for you to right some of these "wrongs" by yourself.

So let's agree there are many things that are wrong. But let's not try to change them except through the ballot box. Let's each of us live within the system, live within our society of law, and use the built-in advantages of our society in such a way that each of us will benefit individually. We will not just overcome. We will succeed. We will triumph.

When you play it safe in a savings account, you're gambling—and losing

Jim Burns doesn't gamble. Like most Americans, he works hard for his salary, and he wants to be sure the money he saves is safe. The safest place Jim knows is the savings account at his local bank. Week after week, he makes his deposits.

Throughout the years, Jim had seen other people make fortunes in stocks, bonds, and real estate. He had also seen some people lose fortunes in investments of that type. But Jim didn't want to gamble to win big or lose big. He sacrificed the chance of high return because of the high risk involved. He was happy to settle for a savings account designed to preserve his principal and pay him a modest return on his money.

For many years, Jim had seen that return come to him in the form of interest, and he could count on its being credited to his account regularly. The growth of his savings, Jim admitted, had been slow, but it had been steady. He was sure he was building a nest egg to finance his retirement, to insure against the cost of illness, to buy a new car or a new home, to provide an umbrella for a rainy day.

Today, as he continues to make his weekly deposits, he's still sure that his money is growing.

But Jim Burns is dead wrong.

So are the millions of other Americans who put their faith

in savings accounts to protect their hard-earned dollars.

The fatal mistake of these thrift-minded people is thinking in terms of dollars and not in terms of what those dollars will buy. These savings acount depositors don't take inflation into account. Because of inflation, *the money in their savings accounts will buy less at the end of the year than at the beginning—despite the interest they're paid.*

Let me show you the facts:

You're getting 4.5 to 5% interest in savings accounts. If you tie your money up in certificates for two to ten years, you're getting 5.75 to 6%. You pay income taxes on this interest, so your net gain is only about 3 to 4%. But while you're earning that 3 to 4% during a year, inflation decreases the value of every dollar you're earning by 6 to 7%. *You're actually losing 2 to 4% on your money every year.* And that loss is compounded annually.

Far from building a nest egg, you're tearing it down. Far from moving ahead, you're going backward. Instead of earning, you're actually *paying* 2 to 4% per year for the "privilege" of *giving* banks the use of your savings—on which the banks make record profits.

To bring home the terrible effects of inflation on your savings, I'd like to tell you the story of a young family that saved up $2,000 twenty-five years ago and deposited it in a savings account. The family planned to use those savings today. The original $2,000 would have grown through twenty-five years of compound interest to about $3,500 (after income taxes on the interest had been deducted). Twenty-five years ago, $2,000 would have covered the family's living expenses for one year. So with $3,500, the family figured that, today, they could live for nearly two years.

But $3,500 today will buy only what $700 would have bought 25 years ago.

The family's nest egg, despite all the money it had earned

in a savings account for a quarter of a century, had shrunk to one-third its *original* value in terms of buying power. By making what it thought to be the safest investment, that family actually threw two-thirds of its money away. The $2,000, which could have bought 12 months' living when it was deposited, can now cover only 4 months'—even though that $2,000 had grown to $3,500 during the 25 years.

Had anyone told them they were gambling when that family deposited its $2,000 in a savings account, they would have been shocked. Yet that family *was* gambling that its money—plus interest, minus income taxes—would buy more tomorrow than it did today. For 25 years that family gambled, and for 25 years that family lost. During the last 5 to 7 years that family lost heavily as the rate of inflation went up sharply. That family's conservative approach to investments was gambling just as surely as is betting on horses.

When *you* place your money in a savings account, you're gambling just as that family did.

But you're not only gambling on the rate of inflation. You're also gambling on the interest rate, which can and does fluctuate: it could go up, it could go down. What are your chances of winning on these twin gambles?

Let's begin with a look at the inflation gamble.

In a "safe" savings account, you're sure of increasing your dollars by 5% less taxes for a net gain of 3 or 3.5%. If inflation runs at a rate higher than your net gain of 3 or 3.5%, your purchasing power decreases. Inflation has been running well over that figure. When you gamble on inflation, the odds are you'll lose.

The interest rate gamble is tied in with inflation.

If inflation gets worse, interest rates may rise. (Twenty years or so ago, interest rates were in the range of only 1 to 1.5%; they gradually rose to 5% as inflation climbed.) But interest rates won't rise fast enough—they never have risen fast enough—to catch up with our rocketing inflation.

If inflation slows, interest rates will drop—so your net gain will still be less than the amount you need to counter inflated prices.

To protect yourself against interest rate decreases, you may be tempted into buying "savings certificates" which offer 5.75 to 6% provided you commit your funds for two to ten years. Because the interest rate is guaranteed, it cannot go down during the term of your certificate.

This may be fine insurance against lower interest rates in the future—provided you're sure that, in the future, rates won't go higher. But you can't be sure. Just a few years ago, hundreds of thousands of people bit at the bait of savings certificate rates of 4.5 to 5% for funds tied up for as long as 15 years. Today's certificates pay 6%, and the people who played it "safe" with the 4.5 to 5% certificates can't trade those certificates for the 6% ones without suffering a sizable loss.

When you buy long-term certificates, you're betting that interest rates will remain steady or go down. But when banks offer higher rates for long-term commitments than for regular accounts, the banks are betting that rates *will* rise in the future. Don't bet against the banks. They hold all the trumps.

So if you're gambling on interest rates to beat inflation, don't. Whether the interest rates go up or down, you always lose.

You can see that when you save your money in the traditional "safe" savings account, your money isn't safe. But, if your "safe" investment is a gamble that doesn't pay off and if speculative investments involve the risk of even greater loss, is there *any* way to protect your nest egg and have it grow safely?

There are *many* ways. These ways involve no greater risk

than that of the "safe" investments which have been and will continue to be sure losers. These ways are detailed for you in the MONEY KEYS to riches in this book. To stop losing and start winning, use these *Keys*.

Money Keys

The safety pin was simple too—
but it made a lot of people rich

Some of the MONEY KEYS in this book are as simple as a safety pin. And as familiar.

But go through them carefully. You may see old facts in a new light—a far more profitable light. You'll begin to realize, *Key by Key,* that the MONEY KEYS are building blocks which, when properly assembled, can increase the return on your savings dramatically.

These building blocks, which may appear simple and not too important, form the necessary foundation for the MONEY KEYS marked TOP SECRET, which can double or triple the income earned on your savings—and in some cases bring you even greater returns.

But observe this caution: These TOP SECRET MONEY KEYS are valuable only if their use is restricted to the readers of this book. So keep these special MONEY KEYS TOP SECRET.

You'll find some MONEY KEYS marked DANGER! Let me tell you why:

Financial institutions of all sorts including the most respectable banks, either purposely or unintentionally, issue statements or place advertisements that tend to mislead the public.

37

The Consumer Affairs Commission of New York City and the Office of the Attorney General of New York State have recently taken notice of this practice—a practice which you might assume would be confined to slick fly-by-nights.

Don't permit yourself to be fooled by misleading information from banks and other financial institutions. If you do, your estate will suffer. Protect your money with the MONEY KEYS marked DANGER!

Money Key No. 2

Increase your interest 11%
by picking the right bank

The advantage:

Banks advertise that they are paying the highest interest rate on savings that the law allows. But there are three kinds of banks, and the highest rate permitted by law for two of them is higher than the highest rate for the third. As this book goes to press, the interest rate ceiling on savings accounts for savings and loan associations and savings banks is 5% per year; for commercial banks it is only 4.5%.

How to use this advantage to make money:

Choose the bank that pays you 5% rather than 4.5%. 5% is more than 11% higher than 4.5%. Here's the arithmetic proof:

$$4.5 \ \%$$
$$\text{plus } 11\% \text{ of } 4.5\% = 0.495\%$$

Total   4.995% (approximately 5%)

Let's understand one thing right off. Increasing an intereset rate from 4.5 to 5% can be described in two ways. It can obviously be properly described as an increase of 0.5%: 4.5% +0.5%=5%. But it can also be described with equal honesty as an 11% interest rate increase simply because 4.5%+11% of

4.5+=5%. I use the second method of calculation for two reasons:

First: The following example demonstrates that this second method of calculation is the one used by major American banks. When these banks decrease a loan interest rate from 9.77% to 8.68%, they do not advertise a decreased interest rate of 1.09%; they advertise a decreased interest rate of 11%. Bankers Trust Company, for instance, claims that you "save up to 11% on our regular annual percentage rate on all Installment Loans of $1,000 or more."

Second, and far more important: If the interest earnings on your savings account at 4.5% yields you $100, at 5% that yield would go up to $111. $111 *is* 11% more than $100. You have increased your dollar interest earnings by 11%, not 0.5%.

You wouldn't turn down an 11% raise. You'd welcome an 11% discount on something you buy. You'd resist an 11% rent increase. Why not take 11% more interest, even if the total gain may be only a few dollars—or even pennies. It's much better in your pocket than in the bank's profits.

You may have already been aware of the higher interest rates paid by savings institutions, but other people are still unaware of it. The New York State Mutual Savings Bank industry is currently spending millions of dollars in advertising to drive home the point that "no commercial bank pays the high interest rate we pay."

But if you have your money in a commercial bank, don't rush off to change banks yet. The money you have in a commercial bank can be used to increase the yield you receive on your savings. In the next section, I'll tell you the story behind this development.

How the banks help you
get a greater return on your savings

You've just finished reading MONEY KEY No. 2, and perhaps you're wondering why two of the three types of banks are permitted to pay an interest rate which is 11% higher than the interest rate permitted the third type of bank. I'd like to tell you about the reason behind this regulation. Then you'll understand why you're justified in getting a better return for your money than that allowed by the legal interest ceiling—and why the banks actually help you get these extra dollars.

I'd like to begin by refreshing your memory concerning the home mortgage industry in the United States. There are vast amounts of money available to finance home mortgages. I am not referring to mortgage funds for big commercial buildings and apartment houses; I am referring only to mortgages for the individually owned home, the owner-occupied type of home—your home and mine. If mortgages weren't available, very few people would be able to own their own homes.

A mortgage is a loan, and you have to pay interest on your home mortgage just as you would on any other type of loan. The cost of most nonmortgage loans from banking institutions run anywhere from 9 to 18% per year. Similar loans from non-banking institutions can exceed 36%. This high cost of funds, if it were applied to the purchase of a home, would be unbearable to the average citizen; he just could not afford to buy a home. He could afford to buy a home only if *low-cost* mortgage funds were made available to him.

But bankers know that their money can earn more from other types of loans than from home mortgages. If bankers can lend their money at from 9 to 18%, why should they lend it at less for home mortgages? If banks were free to lend their money to earn the highest interest, much of that money would *not* be channeled into the home mortgage market. That money would be put to work in the personal loan market, in the business loan market, in the commercial mortgage market—wherever a higher return could be gained.

So two types of banks were authorized by law to provide home mortgages at interest rates the average citizen could afford. These two types of banks are the savings banks and the savings and loan associations. They started early in the nineteenth century. Until recently, the funds of the savings and loan associations have been devoted almost exclusively to home mortgages; currently, regulations permit these funds to be used for other investments as well. Savings banks have always been allowed to invest in fields other than home mortgages.

Now, a bank—whether it's a savings bank, a savings and loan association, or a commercial bank—gets its funds from its depositors. In other words, it's the depositors who provide a bank with the money a bank lends out.

Who are the depositors?

For the average person, a bank is the only practical place to put his money. He could save his cash under the mattress or in the cookie jar, but the bank is a safer place. Depositors in the savings industry are not the very wealthy people, not the corporations, not the businesses. As a matter of fact, in the state of New York the savings bank industry is not permitted to accept a savings account from a business. The overwhelming majority of the funds in the savings industry come from the small savings of the average American.

Savings banks, savings and loan associations, and commercial banks are in competition for these funds. If commercial banks could compete *freely*, they could lure depositors into their banks with offers of much higher interest rates than the savings institutions could afford. Commercial banks would be able to pay 6, 7, or 8% as compared with the savings institutions' 5%.

If commercial banks were permitted to offer these high interest rates, you, the depositor, would take your money out of a savings institution and put it into a commercial bank. There would be no reason why you shouldn't, since in all other respects savings accounts in commercial banks and in savings institutions offer the same advantages, such as availability of funds and federal agency insurance. But if you did transfer your account—and if depositors like you all over the nation did likewise—funds that would have been used by savings institutions to finance home mortgages would be used by commercial banks to finance anything *but* home mortgages.

So you can see why the regulatory agencies of the banking industry order the commercial banks to pay *less* interest than the savings institutions. By keeping the interest rate offered by commercial banks lower than that offered by savings institutions, the regulatory agencies virtually force the average person to put his money into a savings bank or savings and loan association. The result is that there is now about $300 billion in savings institutions. This huge sum is available for low-cost home mortgages. (Interest rates on home mortgages are currently about 7.5%. Not too long ago, the rate was only 4.5%.) By making it difficult for the commercial banks to compete with the savings institutions for the depositor's dollar, the regulatory agencies make certain that the average citizen can get a low-cost home mortgage.

This is fine for the man who needs a home mortgage, but

is it fine for you as a depositor?

Repeat: You have no choice but to put your money into a savings institution, because if you put your savings into a commercial bank, you'd receive less money for it. So, in effect, *you are forced to subsidize the home mortgage industry.* You may be a depositor who holds a home mortgage. Fine! But if you're a depositor and you don't hold a home mortgage, why should *you* be forced to subsidize the home mortgage industry?

There are other industries that are subsidized: farming and aircraft, for example. But these industries are subsidized through tax funds—taxes that are collected from *everyone* in proportion to each citizen's ability to pay. But the home mortgage industry is subsidized only by depositors. The burden of creating home mortgage funds has fallen on *your* back.

Do you realize how heavy that burden is? I've already shown you how, *because of inflation,* the real purchasing power of your savings is less today than it was when you made your deposit a year ago. The man who, last year, put enough money in the bank to live on for 12 months now finds that he can only live for a little more than 11 months on that money— *even with the interest added.* The regulatory agencies keep the interest paid you by savings institutions down to 5% to supply low-cost money to these institutions so that they can afford to offer low-cost home mortgages. But 5% just isn't enough for you to keep up with inflation.

Of course, if you want to use your hard-earned savings to subsidize the home mortgage industry, that's up to you. Settle for 5% if you like—and continue to lose. But if you don't feel that you're under any obligation to subsidize a private industry which exists for the benefit of some but not all of us— then you're justified in searching for ways to get more for your savings dollar. Those two ceilings of 5 and 4.5% are simply unfair to you. So why not do something about it?

The banks *are* doing something about it. And have been

for some time. It was the commercial banks that began the rebellion against these unfair interest ceilings.

Since the end of World War II, the commercial banks have been aggressively pursuing your dollar for *their* savings accounts. They've been doing this by coming up with many new ideas to give you a return on your savings in excess of 4.5% *while still staying within the 4.5% ceiling fixed by law.* As an example, the commercial banks founded the concept of daily interest, which provides an extra yield never before earned on a savings account. Because of many breakthroughs of this nature, commercial banks are now a force to be reckoned with in the savings industry.

As a defensive reaction, the savings institutions have had to take steps to equal or better the offers of the commercial banking industry. In particular, new ideas to get you greater returns on your savings while still staying within the framework of the apparent 5% limitation have come from the savings and loan industry.

But without the competition of the commercial banks, these actions by the savings industry, which benefit you, would never have occurred. Both savings and loan associations and savings banks have always been assured of a steady flow of the nation's savings. As a result, they've become fat and complacent and have tended to offer as little to the depositor as they possibly can. If the savings industry were permitted by regulation to offer more than 5%, the odds are that it would not. It is the savings industry that wants to hold down the interest on your savings. Nevertheless, as long as the commercial banks continue to lure your savings dollars with *new legitimate ways to raise the interest ceilings,* the savings banks and the savings and loan associations will follow suit.

It all adds up to this: the banks—all three types—are actually helping you get more than the legal ceiling on your savings. They're doing this by building advantages into their savings account regulations—for you.

The MONEY KEYS in this book make use of these advantages. With these *Keys*, instead of receiving 4.5 or 5%, you'll receive double that; and in some instances you'll triple or quadruple the established ceilings. And it's all legal. The highest interest rates apparently permitted by law (4.5 and 5%) are no longer the highest interest rates actually permitted by law.

Remember, the banks want your deposits, and they've come up with these built-in advantages in their savings account practices to *get* your deposits. Take advantage of the advantages.

Money Key No. 3

Walk to the bank—
and get your shoes free

The advantage:

There are two major types of savings accounts: the regular savings and the day of deposit to day of withdrawal accounts.

In the regular savings account, interest, no matter when it is compounded, is credited only at the end of some particular period. That period is generally the end of the quarter. If funds are removed prior to the end of the quarter, no interest is earned on those funds for the entire quarter.

In many banks, deposits made in these accounts after the start of the period do not start earning interest until the first of the following month or until the first of the following period. Not infrequently, a depositor is lured by some kind of gift program into opening an account of this type, only to find that funds deposited, say, on January sixteenth didn't start to earn interest until April first—almost three months later.

In the day of deposit to day of withdrawal account, you earn interest for the number of days your money is in the account. For example, you can put your money in on the thirteenth and take it out on the fifteenth, and your money will have earned two days' interest (15 minus 13). Your funds are always available to you. You suffer no penalty if you need money tomorrow and you take the money tomorrow; you'll earn interest through tomorrow.

The day of deposit to day of withdrawal account accepts the idea that when you make a deposit, you're lending money to the bank. When a bank lends *you* money, if you repay the loan in two days, you pay two days' worth of interest. Similarly, when you lend money to a bank, you're entitled to interest for every day you lend that money.

This concept of paying the depositor for every day he leaves money in the bank is a most important breakthrough. Until only a few years ago, the depositor did not receive interest on his funds for every day his funds were on deposit. He received interest only if he kept the funds in until the end of a period.

That period was gradually shortened to attract depositors. The savings and loan industry on the West Coast switched from semiannual interest to quarterly interest and then to monthly interest. It was logical to go one step further and offer daily interest.

But it was a commercial bank, the Chase Manhattan Bank, that pioneered the offer of interest from day of deposit to day of withdrawal. Historically, commercial banks had offered savings accounts more as a convenience to their depositors than as a way for the depositors to make money; interest was minimal. But after World War II, commercial banks realized that individual savings could mount up and become a sizable source of lendable funds. Restricted from offering interest rates competitive with the savings bank and savings and loan industry, commercial banks looked for new ways to attract depositors. Day of deposit to day of withdrawal was an idea that worked for Chase Manhattan, and the practice was followed in short order by a number of other major commercial banks.

The computation of daily interest was a tremendous headache, but as banks became computerized that problem ceased.

Soon, savings and loan associations were offering day of deposit to day of withdrawal accounts. The West Side Federal Savings and Loan Association, based in New York, was the first savings and loan association to adopt the idea of daily interest. Then savings banks, particularly the savings banks of New York State—because they started to lose their depositors to both commercial banks and savings and loan associations—added day of deposit to day of withdrawal accounts to their services.

How to use this advantage to make money:

If you're like most salaried employees, you deposit your paycheck in a checking account and then draw against it for expenses. You'll find it worthwhile instead to deposit the bulk of your paycheck into a day of deposit to day of withdrawal account in a conveniently located bank. Since you can withdraw as often as you like, you can use your savings account very much like a checking account—with one big difference: instead of paying for the account, you *get paid*. Remember, in a day of deposit to day of withdrawal account, you earn interest for every day your money remains in the bank. Until you need your money to pay a bill, your money is making money for you.

How much money? When you deposit a *weekly* paycheck, you're likely to withdraw most of it for expenses during the subsequent week. Until you do, you earn a few days' interest. You earn more interest when you're paid *biweekly* because you can keep your second week's salary in your account for a week plus several days before you have to use it. When you deposit your *monthly* paycheck, you won't get around to using some of your money for three weeks or more, and all that time it's earning interest.

There's a drawback. Using your day of deposit to day of withdrawal account, you must make a trip to the bank to make a withdrawal. You might argue, "Is all this walking to the bank for withdrawals every time I need to pay a bill worth all the shoe leather I use up?"

If you're paid monthly, the additional money you earn in a day of deposit to day of withdrawal account over the course of a year will pay for a new pair of shoes. If you're paid weekly, you'll earn enough to pay for resoling your old shoes. By following the simple actions of this MONEY KEY you may very well *remove the cost* of one of the necessities of your life: by walking to the bank, you can get a pair of shoes *free*. Or at least, get them repaired free.

A small thing? A matter of just pennies or a few dollars. Of course. But pennies or a few dollars are *never* small things. Think of the full rain barrel and remember that it was filled by individual raindrops. Each penny is a raindrop. If on every transaction you can make even one penny, that's one more penny into *your* rain barrel of riches.

Money Key No. 4

Increase your interest
another 12.5%

The advantage:
Many regular savings accounts offer 10 grace days at the
beginning of each quarter. That means money deposited by the
tenth of the first month of each quarter (January, April, July,
October) earns interest from the first of that month.

How to use this advantage to make money:
These grace days can actually increase your rate of interest. You earn interest on funds even when the funds aren't
in the bank, which ends up as a true higher rate of interest.
Here's how it works out:

Deposit your money on the tenth of the first month of any
quarter. It stays on deposit for a total of 80 days, but you receive 90 days worth of interest. That's an increase of 10/80,
or 12.5%, over the normal interest for the quarter.

Assume the interest rate is 5%: 12% of 5% is 0.6%. During
the 80 days your money was on deposit, you earned 5% plus
0.6%, or 5.6%. That's your *true yield* over those 80 days. Although the quoted interest rate remains the same 5%, by taking
advantage of the 10 extra interest days every 3 months, you get
a true yield each 3 months which exceeds the rate quoted by
the banks. Remember, the quoted interest rate is not nearly

51

as important as the yield.

In MONEY KEY NO. 2, I showed you that 5% is really 11% more than 4.5%. In this *Key*, I've gone one step further—to a true yield of 5.6%—and that's 12.5% more than 5%.

You might say "The difference between 4.5 and 5% is only 0.5%—it doesn't mean a thing. And the difference between 5 and 5.6% is only 0.6%—it doesn't mean a thing either."

But those small differences *do* mean a great deal when you figure your total interest earnings over the course of the year. Let's say you earn $100. Increase $100 by 11%—that's the difference between 4.5 and 5%—and you get $111. Then increase that $111 by another 12.5%—that's the difference between 5 and 5.6%—and that $111 grows close to $125.

So you see that although these percentage jumps are small, there is really a big difference between earning $100 interest in the course of a year and earning $125. When you get to the point where your interest is going to be $1,000, then these little percentage jumps make the difference between $1,000 and $1,250. Once again, although the transactions might appear to be worth only pennies, they can add up.

On the other hand, a 12.5% increase may sound like a lot. It would be if this increase applied to all of your funds all the time. But it doesn't. This 12.5% increase applies only to those funds that are deposited on the tenth and kept in for 80 days. This does not increase the annual yield on your savings to any great extent. Nevertheless, small as it may be, you'll earn more interest this way than if your funds had been deposited in an account not offering grace days—and every penny earned is a penny saved.

Far more important: get used to taking advantage of grace days. Later MONEY KEYS will show you how to use them to build sizable annual returns.

TOP SECRET
Money Key No. 5

Earn 7.5%—short term

In the field of finance, it is important to be able to invest money for short terms, even for one day, and earn as much as possible on your investment. Treasury bills, traded on the open market, are examples of short-term instruments. Pick up *The Wall Street Journal, The New York Times,* or the financial page of your local newspaper, and you'll see yields figured on Treasury bills for 11 months, 29 days, and all the way down to a day.

The yield on a Treasury bill today that comes due tomorrow—the yield when you invest your money for only one day—may be 3.8% or 4.1% or somewhere in that neighborhood depending on the current market. The yield is given as an annual percentage rate. So for a safe investment for a day, your yield will actually be less than the 5% you can get from a savings account. This low yield is generally typical of other short-term instruments as well.

But you can get tremendously high yields over short terms by the proper use of savings acounts. This MONEY KEY provides one example.

The advantage:

When a bank offers grace days at the beginning of the quarter, only funds deposited up through, say, January tenth would earn interest from January first. If you deposit money on February tenth, you earn interest only from February tenth.

Some banks, however, offer grace days *every* month. Interest is paid from the first of every month on deposits received through the tenth of that month.

How to use this advantage to make money:

Look for the bank that offers monthly grace days. Deposit funds in a normal 5% account on the tenth of the *last* month of the quarter; say, March tenth.

The funds you deposited earn a full month's interest in two-thirds of a month. The true yield on those funds for that two-thirds of a month is just about 50% higher than the nominal yield of 5%. It's about 7.5%.

Money Key No. 6

A rare opportunity to earn 15%

The advantage:
There are some banks or savings and loan associations that have offered more than 10 grace days each month. As an example, in the state of Maryland, some savings institutions have offered 20 grace days each month.

How to use this advantage to make money:
Look for a bank or savings and loan association that offers more than 10 grace days each month. There may be banks or savings and loan associations in your neighborhood offering 15 or even 20 grace days each month. That means you can make deposits up through the twentieth of each month and earn interest from the first.

Banks or savings and loan associations offering more than 10 grace days are extremely rare. If you're one of the lucky few who may find a bank or savings and loan association that offers 20 grace days each month, your true yield on money deposited on the twentieth of the last month in the quarter will be about 200% higher than the nominal interest rate. On a nominal 5% account, money deposited, say, on June twentieth and withdrawn on June thirtieth would have earned 30 days' interest in 10 days, providing a true yield of 15%.

Because it's so unusual to find more than 10 grace days each month, in future calculations on this subject, we'll figure on only 10 grace days.

DANGER!
Money Key No. 7

Watch out for
banks that don't offer grace days

Remember: A regular savings account has an advantage over a day of deposit to day of withdrawal account only if it offers grace days.

Don't be fooled by the newspaper and radio advertising of some banks which boast that your interest is credited monthly but which end their sales pitch without offering grace days.

For example, the president of the Provident Savings Bank in Jersey City, N.J., wrote to my wife in response to her query about the bank's radio advertising:

"Thank you for taking the time to inquire about our regular savings account. Provident pays 5% per year from day of deposit, credited and compounded monthly. Deposits start earning dividends from the moment received. Dividends are posted on the last business day of each and every month."

But no mention is made of grace days.

This type of account must be evaluated against the day of deposit to day of withdrawal account. The day of deposit to day of withdrawal account is superior to the monthly account that offers no grace days.

Grace days are powerful tools that can earn more money for you. Be sure you're getting them when you open a regular account.

DANGER!
Money Key No. 8

Watch out for
banks that pay interest only semiannually

Recap: In general, there are two types of savings accounts—the regular account and the day of deposit to day of withdrawal account. Both types of accounts will be useful to you in getting more from your savings dollar. So don't dismiss the regular savings account.

But in selecting a regular savings account, be careful. Some banks pay only semiannually. This means that, should you make a withdrawal before the end of the semiannual period, you could lose more than five months' worth of accrued interest.

One rule in selecting a regular account is this: Choose the account from which you can withdraw money in the shortest period of time without losing interest. Use the regular savings account that offers you quarterly interest rather than semiannual interest. If a bank offers monthly interest, pick that bank over one offering quarterly interest—provided it offers grace days and bonus days, which I'll tell you about shortly.

Exception to the rule: Oddly enough, one account that pays interest only semiannually—and at the rate of only 4.5% at that—may turn out to be one of the most profitable accounts you ever put your savings into. You'll find the details later in this book.

DANGER!
Money Key No. 9

Watch out for
free gifts for $5,000 deposits

Banks and savings and loan associations are permitted by the regulatory agencies to spend $10 for a gift given in exchange for a deposit of $5,000. Since these financial institutions buy their gifts wholesale and in large quantities, the items given away are usually worth between $15 and $20 to the consumer.

When you accept one of these $15 to $20 gifts, you agree to tie up your $5,000 for 14 months at only 5%. You could, since you're willing to tie up your money, put your $5,000 in a two-year savings certificate at 6% instead. Let's see which choice is better for you.

The bank is paying out $10 when you accept the gift. On $5,000 for 14 months, it's less than 1/5 of 1% per year. If you figure your gain not on the $10 that the bank paid for the gift but on the value of the gift to you, at the most $20, you increase your yield by less than 2/5 of 1%. Your total yield comes to slightly less than 5.2 or 5.4% based respectively on the cost or value of the gift.

On the other hand, when you tie your money up in a two-year certificate, you get 6% plus 1/5 to 2/5% over two years in cost or value to you of the gift, which equals 1/10 or 2/10% per year for a total yield of 6.1 to 6.2% per year (as compared to 5.2 to 5.4%—0.8 to 0.9% more than your greatest possible yield for accepting a gift to tie up your money for 14 months.

Accepting a gift in return for a deposit of $5,000 is not the most profitable way to save your money.

TOP SECRET

Money Key No. 10

Get ten bank gifts intead of one

The advantage:

Many people are tempted to put money into savings accounts to get what they think are gifts. They're *not* gifts—not things given free. They're a return of value for a service rendered to the banks by *you*. That service is depositing your money and leaving it on deposit for a certain length of time. Giving you a gift is the same as paying you. Indeed, some banks will give you a gift check if you prefer it.

How to use this advantage to make money:

In the MONEY KEY you just read, you discovered that a bank spends about $10 for the gift it gives you in return for a $5,000 deposit.

When you deposit 1/10 of that amount, $500, you can also get a gift. On $500 accounts, a bank is allowed by the regulatory agencies to spend $5 on a gift. In return for that gift, you tie your $500 up for 14 months. The actual retail value of the gifts a bank pays $5 for is close to $10. If you figure your yield on the retail value, you're getting about an extra 2%. If you put your money in at 5%, the gift brings your yield up to around 7%.

There's a way of using gifts to get even more than 7% on a $500 deposit. After two months in a day of deposit to day of withdrawal account, transfer your $500 into a one-year certificate at 5.75%. (If necessary, deposit enough extra money in your account to meet the bank's minimum requirements and keep the account open.) You'll find you're getting better than an average of 7.5%, and that's a good return.

Caution: Find out whether *your* bank will permit you to make the transfer.

Some banks offer gifts for deposits of a little as $50 provided the $50 stays in the account for 14 months. The banks pay $2 or possibly $2.50 for these gifts, but the retail value is close to $5. That $5 amounts to almost 9% interest. That's in addition to the 5% interest you'd get normally. Add these two figures, and you see that *you get a 14% return for your $50 deposit*.

The smaller the deposit, the greater your advantage in taking a gift. If you put $500 into ten $50 accounts, taking 10 gifts —one gift for every $50—you'd get far more return for your money than by taking one gift on a $500 account. Even if you sold the gifts at a discount, you could certainly get $30 for the 10 of them. That's about $10 more value to you than the value of a gift from a $500 account.

Money Key No. 11

Withdraw your money—
and continue to earn interest on it

The advantage:
Bonus days. These are the days before the end of the quarter or interest-paying period during which money can be withdrawn without loss of interest.

Bonus days are usually given in addition to grace days on regular savings accounts.

How to use this advantage to make money:
If you have your choice between a bank that offers bonus days plus grace days and one that offers only grace days, choose the bank that gives you the bonus days as well.

Many banks give you three bonus days. In those banks, the funds you withdraw during the last three business days of the quarter earn for the full quarter. Since the last three business days of a month often include a weekend, you'll frequently receive five days of additional interest if you withdraw your money five calendar days (three business days) before the end of the quarter. For those five days, you're actually earning money on money that's no longer in the bank.

Bonus days are unimportant if money remains *in* the bank. But if funds are going to be either used or transferred, five days of extra interest is a valuable asset. Remember this asset, because we're going to make use of it in later MONEY KEYS to boost your yield substantially.

Enjoy life more
while building an estate

You're using found money to build your estate with the MONEY
KEYS. That's money saved by resisting the temptation to buy
and buy and buy. Strange as it may seem, saving money that
way can really add to the enjoyment of life. I'd like to give
you a personal example.

I had a friend in the liquor business. He used to select good
wines for me at low prices. From time to time, my wife and I
would open a bottle and enjoy it. Usually we'd wait for an opportunity to share the bottle with another couple rather than
drink it all ourselves. That added to the enjoyment. Having
wine was a special occasion, and I looked forward to it.

Then my wife and I went to Europe for 30 days, and the
wine flowed like water. With the wines, there were wonderful
adventures in food. I love adventures in food, so I overate. I
didn't overdrink—I've never been inebriated in my life; but I
did drink wine, as most Europeans do, with lunch and with
dinner every day. Between the overeating and the constant
drinking, before our 30 days were up, my stomach became so
sour that I lost the taste for wine.

Today—and this is 16 or 17 years later—that taste is still
lost. Oh, on rare occasions, I will enjoy a glass of wine, but I
don't get anything like the degree of enjoyment that I did be-

fore I became a glutton on that European vacation. Those wonderful times with my wife or with another couple over a bottle of wine are gone forever. By satiating myself twice a day every day with wine, I spoiled something wonderful for the rest of my life. By thinking I would enjoy myself, I ruined one form of enjoyment forever.

I learned a lesson: Don't overdo any kind of pleasure; it will turn sour on you. Take just enough pleasure, and you'll enjoy it more and you'll enjoy it longer.

When you resist the temptation to buy, buy, buy, what you *do* buy gives you greater pleasure than if you had given in to temptation. The solid citizen who purchases a suit after having bought no suits for three years gets far more enjoyment out of anticipating that suit, shopping for that suit, deciding on that suit, and finally wearing that suit, than the fashion-minded individual who gets another suit with every change of style and every change of season.

The mature person who resists the temptation to buy, buy, buy in order to find the money to save has another great pleasure in store for him: the joy of building money. There's no happiness like that of the man who is watching his estate grow.

Savings accounts at 5%
pay you more than
savings certificates at 5.25 to 6.27%

At this point, I should like to discuss some of the other instruments available at banks—because these instruments *do* pay more than savings accounts—and I'd like to compare the advantages of these instruments with the advantages of savings accounts. When I've finished my discussion, I think you'll have the answer to the question: "Why should I put my money in a savings acount at 5% when I can put it in a time-deposit certificate paying much more?"

Let's take a look at the type of instruments now being offered:

The 90-day Savings Certificate. Regulations permit savings banks and savings and loan associations to pay 5.25% on this instrument. You cannot take your money out for 90 days without losing all the accrued interest.

In a regular savings account with interest paid quarterly, if you withdraw your money before the end of the quarter, you lose the accrued interest. That disadvantage is the same as that of the 90-day savings certificate. So, you may wonder, why keep money in a regular savings account that pays only 5% when you can get 5.25% on a 90-day savings certificate?

First, most of the banks and savings and loan associations don't promote these 90-day instruments. They do promote the one-year and two-year certificates, which I'll get to shortly. You may have a difficult time finding a 90-day savings certificate.

In addition, there are no grace or bonus days on the 90-day savings certificate. Since you can get 5% in a savings account for keeping your money in for only 80 out of 90 days by using the grace days or by keeping your money in even less than 80 days by using grace and bonus days (I'll explain that later on), you'll find that the actual effective rate in a savings account is just about the same 5.25% as that offered by a 90-day savings certificate. There's really no advantage in tying up your money.

The 180-day Savings Certificate. Regulations permit savings banks and savings and loan associations to pay 5.5% on these time deposits. Your money is tied up for six months. If you take your money out *before* three months are over, you lose *all* the accrued interest. If you take your money out *after* three months are over, you lose *three* months of your interest.

If you know you're not going to need the money and you have no other way to play with it, of course 5.5% is better than the 5% you'd get in a savings account. And certainly the rates on one-year and long-term savings certificates, described in the next two paragraphs, are also better.

The One-year Savings Certificate. This certificate ties up your money for one year, but you earn 5.75%.

Long-term Savings Certificates. Some people, with a chunk of money that is already saved and is just going to sit in the bank, are likely to invest that money in savings certificates for terms longer than a year at 6%. (These savings certificates are available for terms of from two to ten years.) In some banks where these certificates are continuously compounded (which is the subject of a later MONEY KEY), the yield is 6.27%

The interest rates I've quoted on savings certificates are

offered only by savings banks and savings and loan associations. Commercial banks are restricted by regulations to paying 0.25% less than the other two types of banks. For example, on a two-year certificate, savings banks and savings and loan associations can offer 6%, but commercial banks can offer only 5.75%.

If you're a large depositor, though, you might find it to your advantage to make use of a savings certificate in a commercial bank. (By the way, a commercial bank calls instruments of this type "certificates of deposit.") If you have $100,000 or more to put aside for a few years, commercial banks are permitted to pay you 7.5%. Although savings and loan associations are permitted to pay you this rate, many will not.

Obviously, the small investor is best off placing his savings in a savings bank or a savings and loan association. That's exactly what the regulatory agencies intended—to force the little guy, not the big guy, to subsidize the home mortgage market.

On the surface, most savings certificates look like better investments than most savings accounts. Let's look beneath the surface.

So far as all savings certificates are concerned, there is always a penalty: you tie up your money. Although you can cash in your savings certificates, you lose interest when you do. You *can* receive the interest quarterly. Or you can let the interest accrue until the end of the time deposit. But either way your principal is tied up.

To some people, savings certificates offer this advantage: If you buy, say, a four-year savings certificate, you know exactly what you'll be getting in interest for the next four years. Your interest earnings are not affected by changes in the general interest rates on savings. General interest rates may go down, but *your* rates remain steady. On the other hand, if general interest rates go up, you're stuck with the lower interest rate.

You must remember also that you have to pay annual income taxes on the interest, and the rate of interest of most savings certificates is insufficient to keep the value of your nest egg from going downward due to inflation.

From the viewpoint of interest rates, savings certificates do look more attractive than savings accounts. But before running out to put your entire nest egg or even a major part of it into savings certificates, I would suggest that you consider using the knowledge that you'll gain from this book. You'll find that by the proper use of regular savings accounts, your actual return can be much greater than that which you'd get from savings certificates. In a matter of days or a couple of weeks, you may double or triple your interest rates—and in some cases get even higher returns. And—your funds will always be available to you.

The important thing is to make sure that—no matter how small your nest egg—it's going forward, not backward. You do that when you follow the MONEY KEYS in this book. But when you settle for savings certificates because using the MONEY KEYS requires a little work, you're saying, "I resign myself to the fact that the value of my savings is going downward." Think about that, and you'll agree that the amount of work involved in going back and forth to banks to carry out the directions of the MONEY KEYS is well worthwhile.

Money Key No. 12

How to use **two** savings accounts
to earn extra money

The advantages:

Let's review the advantages of the regular savings account with grace days and bonus days and the day of deposit to day of withdrawal account without grace and bonus days.

In the regular savings account with grace days and bonus days, *you can earn interest on money which is not in your account.* You can earn interest from the first of the month even if you deposit your money on the tenth. You can withdraw funds three business days—which is often five calendar days— before the end of the quarter and earn money on the funds you've withdrawn.

In a day of deposit to day of withdrawal account, you don't lose any interest if you have to withdraw your funds before the end of the interest-paying period. If you make that kind of withdrawal on your regular account, you lose your interest.

How to use these advantages to make money:

Open both types of accounts and combine the advantages of each. Here's how to do it:

Use your day of deposit to day of withdrawal account to meet your everyday needs. Also use it as your emergency account. You can withdraw the money from this account without any loss of interest. Had you drawn funds from your regular account before the end of the interest period, you would have lost interest. Using your day of deposit to day of withdrawal account in this way *saves you money*.

Use your regular account to deposit savings during the first 10 days, or whatever the grace period is, of any month— and earn that extra interest from the first. This *makes you money* you would not have made had you deposited your funds in your day of deposit to day of withdrawal account. Remember, in a day of deposit to day of withdrawal account, savings deposited on the tenth earn money from the tenth, not from the first.

In short, during the grace-day period, make deposits in your regular account to earn extra interest. After the grace-day period, make deposits in your day of deposit to day of withdrawal account. The money you make and the money you save by using two accounts instead of one adds up to *extra* money for your estate.

TOP SECRET
Money Key No. 13

How to make two savings accounts
pay interest at the same time
—on the same money

The advantages:
Grace days. Bonus days. Day of deposit to day of withdrawal accounts.

How to use these advantages to make money:
STEP No. 1. Maintain two savings accounts: a regular savings account with grace and bonus days and a day of deposit to day of withdrawal account.

STEP No. 2. Withdraw funds from your regular savings account three business days before the end of the quarter. You continue to earn money on the money you've withdrawn during those bonus days—and perhaps on two more days if a weekend is added to the bonus days.

STEP No. 3. Take the money you've withdrawn from your regular account and place it into your day of deposit to day of withdrawal account. *Now, for three to five days, your money is earning interest in both accounts.*

STEP No. 4. Keep the money in your day of deposit to day of withdrawal account until the tenth of the month. On the tenth of the month, remove your money from your day of de-

72

posit to day of withdrawal account and place it into your regular savings account. *Now the same money which had been earning interest for 10 days (the first to tenth) in your day of deposit to day of withdrawal account earns money for the same 10 days (grace days) in your regular account.*

With the same funds, you now have been earning money in two savings accounts for a total of 13 or 14 days (bonus days plus grace days). If your regular savings account offers 20 grace days, you could earn money on two accounts with the same funds for as much as 23 to 24 days out of the month.

You can earn 5% on one account and 5% on another— with the same money. Simply by maintaining two types of savings accounts and making withdrawal from one and deposits into the other as described in this MONEY KEY, *you can get 10% on your savings for at least 13 days of each quarter.*

Slowly but surely your rain barrel of riches will fill. Forthcoming MONEY KEYS may make it overflow.

TOP SECRET

Money Key No. 14

Earn 10% on your savings
—without tying up your money

In the previous MONEY KEY, I told you how to earn 10% on your savings by shuttling your funds between your day of deposit to day of withdrawal account and your regular account with grace and bonus days.

That *Key* had this disadvantage: Money withdrawn from your day of deposit to day of withdrawal account and deposited in your regular savings account on the tenth day of the first month of the quarter cannot be withdrawn again until the end of the quarter without loss of interest.

Example: The end of a quarter is March 31. The bonus days begin on March 29, or on March 27 if there's a weekend splitting up the last three business days of the month. You withdraw from your regular savings account and place the amount withdrawn into your day of deposit to day of withdrawal account on March 27 or 29. On April 10, you withdraw that deposit and redeposit it in your regular savings account. When you do this, you tie up that money in your regular savings account until the end of June, since withdrawal before then means the loss of interest.

Remember though, that money in your day of deposit to

day of withdrawal account can be withdrawn at any time *without* loss of interest. Also remember that many banks offer grace days *every* month. You can put these two advantages together to earn 10% on your money without tying up your funds for most of the quarter.

How to use these advantages to make money:

STEP No. 1. Carry out Steps No. 1 through 3 of the previous MONEY KEY, *How to Make Two Savings Accounts Pay Interest at the Same Time—on the Same Money.*

STEP No. 2. Do *not* carry out Step No. 4 of MONEY KEY No.13. That is to say, do not withdraw the money from your day of deposit to day of withdrawal account on the tenth of the first month of the quarter.

STEP No. 3. Keep the money in your day of deposit to day of withdrawal account until the tenth of the *last* month of the quarter. *Until* that date, your money is available to you every day without loss of interest. *On* the tenth of the last month of the quarter, transfer your money into your regular savings account.

During that last month, you have already earned 10 days' interest in your day of deposit to day of withdrawal account. When you transfer your funds on the tenth (see DANGER MONEY KEY No. 18), you earn 10 days' interest on the same funds in your regular account. You've now earned 10% on your money for 13 or 14 days (bonus days *plus* grace days in the last month). Your funds are tied up only for the rest of the last month, since interest accrues at the end of the month.

Example: On Wednesday, December 27, withdraw funds from your regular account and deposit it in your day of deposit to day of withdrawal account. This gives you 10% interest on the same funds in *both* accounts for 5 bonus days. Do *not* transfer the funds back to your regular account on January 10 (the first month of the quarter). Hold the funds in your day of deposit to day of withdrawal account until Friday, March 9 (the last month of the quarter). You earn 10% on your funds for another 9 days—the first 9 days in March.

Your money is tied up only from March 10 through 28—or about half a month. In return for tying up your money for only about 15 days, you've made double interest.

TOP SECRET

Money Key No. 15

How to get 13 months' interest per year

In the last two MONEY KEYS, Nos. 13 and 14, I showed you how to earn 10% on your savings at the beginning of a quarter and at the end of a quarter. Can you do it in the middle of a quarter? YES, YOU *CAN.*

The advantages:
Regular accounts with grace days. Day of deposit to day of withdrawal accounts.

How to use these advantages to make money:
STEP No. 1. Maintain two accounts—a day of deposit to day of withdrawal account and a regular savings account with grace days *each month.*
STEP No. 2. February 1 is the middle of a quarter. On that date, deposit your money into your day of deposit to day of withdrawal account.
STEP No. 3. On February 10, withdraw that money. You've earned interest through the tenth.
STEP No. 4. On the tenth, take the money you withdrew and deposit it into your regular account. You earn interest for

the 10 grace days from the first of the month.

In this way, you've earned double interest on your money from the first through the tenth—10% rather than 5%. You can do this four times a year, giving you more than a month's extra interest. In one year, you can earn more than 13 months' interest.

Variation: Instead of using a day of deposit to day of withdrawal account and a regular account with grace days, use *two* day of deposit to day of withdrawal accounts with grace days. (See MONEY KEY No. 16.)

It's your money,
make it grow for **you**
—not for the banks

Some people may feel a little uneasy, even a little guilty, about using these MONEY KEYS. These people are hesitant to do anything out of the ordinary. As a matter of fact, these people often feel guilty when they go into a bank to withdraw their own money. And many banks *make* them feel guilty. At some banks, tellers actually ask the depositors "*Why* are you withdrawing this money?" Believe it or not!

So far as feeling guilty about using these MONEY KEYS is concerned, remember that the banks make so much money out of your money that they don't know what to do with it. All you have to do to prove that to yourself is walk down any major avenue of any city and look at the bank buildings. Magnificent new skyscrapers—how rich-looking they are! In each bank, there are thousands of square feet of space for every person who enters. Bankers build these huge palaces as monuments to themselves. Billions of dollars are squandered on these structures. Bankers are able to do this because *you* are forced to give the banks your money at very low rates.

Yes, *forced*. Banking is a legally mandated monopoly—an entire industry controlled by thirteen men in three federal agencies—the seven governors of the Federal Reserve Board and the three members each of the Federal Home Loan Bank

Board and the Federal Deposit Insurance Corporation—all of whom are bankers or friends of bankers. It is this control of *your* savings by a handful of men that makes the multibillion-dollar display of financial palaces possible.

So don't feel guilty if you learn that instead of making 5% for lending your money to a bank, you can really make 10, 12, 15, or 20%—and more. The banking business won't fail if you do. It won't even feel the effects of your action, because most people will still put in their money at 4.5, 5, or 6%. The fact that you take advantage of banking regulations to make more money for yourself will not make any difference at all to the banking industry. But the difference to you will be enormous. Let me emphasize a point I've made before: If you put your money in at the advertised rates, the value of your money goes backward, because inflation is eating away the buying power of your dollar. But when you double or triple those advertised rates, the value of your money will grow; and the total value of your estate will grow.

YES, YOU *CAN* save more. YES, YOU *CAN* build an estate faster. Use the MONEY KEYS with pride and with dignity—and with the assurance that what you're doing is not only right—it's necessary.

TOP SECRET
Money Key No. 16

Gain an extra half-month's interest
each quarter

The advantages:

The advantages of the regular savings account are the grace and bonus days, but these accounts don't give you the advantage of interest from day of deposit to day of withdrawal. The usual day of deposit to day of withdrawal account offers no grace or bonus days.

There is a type of account which combines the advantages of both grace and bonus days and interest from day of deposit to day of withdrawal. This type of account is available at West Side Federal Savings in New York, Great Western Savings in California, and Prudential Savings in Utah as well as at scores of other savings and loan associations.

Let me spell out the advantages of this type of "combined" account:

* Funds earn interest from day of deposit to day of withdrawal.
* Funds deposited by the tenth of any month earn interest from the first of that month provided those funds remain in the institution until the end of the quarter.
* Funds may be withdrawn up to three business days be-

fore the end of the quarter without loss of interest.

I don't know of any savings or commercial bank that offers this combined account.

How to use these advantages to make money:

If you put the three bonus days and ten grace days each month to use, you'll be earning about an extra half-month's interest each quarter on this type of day of deposit to day of withdrawal account.

If there is no savings and loan association nearby offering a combined account, there is no reason why you shouldn't open such an account by mail. Banking by mail has become so widespread that you need not be afraid to send funds to any federally insured institution, whether it's in the next county, the next borough, the next town—or across many state lines. I live in New York, and I've kept accounts in California and Nevada for years.

In a combined account, you have to be careful about one thing. I'll tell you what that is in the DANGER MONEY KEY that follows.

DANGER!
Money Key No. 17

Watch out for
loss of interest on some
day of deposit to day of withdrawal accounts

The disadvantages:

If you make a deposit on January 10 in a day of deposit to day of withdrawal account which offers 10 grace days, your money will earn interest from January 1 provided that the money remains in the account until the end of March.

Suppose, though, you need funds before the end of March —which funds are you taking out, the funds you just put in or the funds you already had in? The answer is the funds you just put in. So those funds did *not* earn interest from January 1. This banking practice is known as "last in, first out."

Let me give you an example. Let's say you had $1,000 in your account and on January 10 you put in an additional deposit of $500. If you were to withdraw $200 on February 15, the bank would figure that $200 as having been withdrawn from your last deposit of $500. You lose the 10 extra days' interest on that $200.

How to get rid of these disadvantages:

To prevent loss of interest, maintain two accounts of the same kind in the same bank, one in your name and one in your name in trust for your wife or child or in your name and your wife's (a joint account). Make your withdrawals from the account that has *all* its funds in from the beginning of the quarter. Make your deposits into the second account, and take advantage of the grace days.

DANGER!
Money Key No. 18

Watch out for
losing interest by transferring funds

The disadvantage:

In MONEY KEYS Nos. 13 and 14, I showed you how, by maintaining two different accounts in the same bank—a day of deposit to day of withdrawal account and a regular account—you can earn double interest for a short period. In MONEY KEY No. 17, I showed you how to use two accounts (day of deposit to day of withdrawal) to minimize loss of interest on withdrawals before the end of interest periods.

But what I told you to do won't work if you tell your bank to *transfer* your funds. That's because when a bank transfers from one of your accounts to another, the bank pays interest on only *one* account.

How to get rid of the disadvantage:

Make an actual withdrawal from one account. Then deposit what you withdrew into the other account. By this simple procedure, you can be reasonably assured of making interest on both accounts.

Money Key No. 19

Increase your interest rate by another 4%

The advantage:

I've discussed different types of compounding with you—from annual to daily. The most recent type of compounding is called "continuous compounding." I'd like to explain it.

Assume a $100 deposit. At a 5% interest rate compounded *annually*, your $100 earns $5 in interest by the end of the year. Your yield is 5%. *Compounded semiannually*, your $100 at 5% earns $5.06. Your yield is 5.06%. *Compounded quarterly*, your $100 at 5% earns $5.09. Your yield is 5.09%.

You can see that the more often your money is compounded, the greater your yield becomes. But if you study those figures, you'll note that with each *increase* in compounding, the increase in yield becomes *smaller*. When compounding is doubled—from once a year to twice a year (annually to semiannually)—the yield goes up 0.06% (from 5 to 5.06%); but when twice-a-year compounding is doubled (semiannually to quarterly), the yield rises only 0.03% (5.06 to 5.09%). Let's go one step further:

Instead of doubling the compounding quarterly, let's multiply the number of compondings in a quarter by 90. That brings us to *daily compounding*. Despite the large increase in compounding, your yield increases only 0.04% over that of quarterly compounding (5.09 to 5.13%).

Nevertheless, your yield *does* rise because of the increase in the number of times your money is compounded. Suppose a bank switched from daily to hourly compounding. Your yield would increase slightly. If the bank went from hourly compounding to compounding every minute, then to every second, your yield would continue to go up by small amounts. And if the bank went on to compound a thousand times a second, then a million times a second, then a billion times a second, the yield would rise a bit more. The highest yield from compounding that you can get is when your money is compounded continuously.

Mathematicians have worked out a formula for calculating continuous compounding, and it's this formula that's fed into the computers. As a result of continuous compounding, your money at 5% gives you a yield of 5.2%. That's 0.07% more than the yield of 5.13% from daily compounding.

How to use this advantage to make money:

On $100 in the bank, the whole difference at the end of the year between compounding annually and compounding continuously is only 20 cents ($5 to $5.20). Some people sneer, "Oh, why trouble, the amount is so small." They point out that even if you have $10,000 in the bank, at the end of the year instead of receiving $500 at 5%, you receive $520—"And what's the big deal?"

Granted $20 is not a tremendous amount. But it's $20 you wouldn't otherwise have. And remember, when $5 goes to $5.20, your interest rate has increased by 4%.

So everything else being equal—grace days, bonus days, and other built-in advantages—if one bank offers quarterly compounding, another bank offers daily compounding, and another bank offers continuous compounding, choose the bank that offers continuous compounding.

TOP SECRET
Money Key No. 20

Make 9.5% on your money over any weekend

The advantages:

Many commercial banks remain open after 3 P.M. But as soon as 3 P.M. passes, these banks change the date of all transactions to the following banking day. A transaction made after 3 P.M. on Thursday is dated Friday. A transaction made after 3 P.M. on Friday is dated Monday or, if Monday is a holiday, Tuesday.

In short, if you make a deposit in or a withdrawal from a commercial bank on Friday after 3 P.M., the bank records your deposit or withdrawal as of the following Monday or, if Monday is a holiday, Tuesday.

So, if you withdraw money from your savings account in a commercial bank on Friday after 3 P.M., that money continues to earn interest until the next following business day, which would be Monday or, in the case of a Monday holiday, Tuesday. *So you've picked up three or four additional days of interest after you've actually withdrawn your money.*

Let's leave commercial banks for a moment and turn to savings banks and savings and loan associations. Many have evening hours every business day. Almost all stay open on Friday evenings, particularly in residential, metropolitan, and suburban areas. But there's a difference between the post-3 P.M. banking practices of these banks and those of commercial banks.

Most savings banks and savings and loan associations do *not* record transactions made after 3 P.M. as of the following banking day. As long as these banks are open on any day, transactions are entered as of that day. If you make a deposit on Friday in a day of deposit to day of withdrawal account, then your interest begins on Friday.

How to use these advantages to make money:

STEP No. 1. Open up a day of deposit to day of withdrawal account in a commercial bank and in a nearby savings bank or savings and loan association.

STEP No. 2. On Friday after 3 P.M., *withdraw* a sum of money from your commercial bank savings account. Since the withdrawal will be entered in the bank's records as occurring on the next banking day, which is Monday or Tuesday, you will be earning 4.5% over the weekend on the money you withdrew.

STEP No. 3. On the same day, deposit the money you withdrew into your savings bank or savings and loan association account. Since the deposit is entered on Friday, you'll be earning 5% on that deposit over the weekend.

So, over the weekend, the same sum of money is earning interest in *two* banks. One bank pays 4.5% and the other 5%, for a total of 9.5%.

Can you earn 9.5% on the *same* money *every* weekend? YES, YOU *CAN*.

Let's continue with the example I've just given you. On Friday, you deposited a sum in your savings bank or savings and loan association account. At any time during the following week (except Friday), withdraw that sum and redeposit it in your commercial bank savings account. As long as your accounts are day of deposit to day of withdrawal, you lose no interest by this transaction. On Friday, repeat Steps No. 1 to 3.

In this way, you can earn 9.5% on some of your savings for a minimum of 3 days a week for 52 weeks—a total of 156 days. The number of legal holidays falling on Monday could increase this total to 160 days or more.

Other MONEY KEYS make yields higher than 9.5% available for longer periods than weekends, so it's not necessary to use this *Key* all the time. Use this MONEY KEY when you can't use any other MONEY KEY offering you a greater return.

I'm often asked, "Won't the banks object to repeated shuttling of funds?" The concept under which banks have been selling the day of deposit to day of withdrawal accounts is this: "We will accept anyone's money for as long as he's willing to leave it with us, and he may remove it any time." Prove it to yourself by reading any bank's advertisement soliciting day of deposit to day of withdrawal accounts.

I have moved money out of and into accounts constantly over many years and I have never received one word of objection.

TOP SECRET

Money Key No. 21

Double your interest
190 days a year

You can earn 10% at the beginning and end of each quarter for 13 to 14 days. That's 52 to 56 days a year. (See MONEY KEYS No. 13 and 14.)

On every weekend in which your money is not tied up earning 10%, you can earn 9.5%. That's 44 weekends, which, including legal holidays, comes to about 136 days. (See MONEY KEY No. 20.)

By the careful placement of funds, you can virtually double your interest for about 190 days a year!

But it does take a good many visits to your banks. Is it worth the trouble?

It's really not that much trouble. Many people go to their banks a couple of times a week anyway. These are people who don't want to carry around a lot of money; they're afraid of losing it or being robbed. Or these are people who want to earn the maximum interest on their money. When sizable sums of money are involved—say, savings accounts from $10,000 and up—making trips like these to your banks *in order to virtually double your interest for the majority of days of the year* becomes very worthwhile.

But even when sizable sums aren't involved, remember you're filling your rain barrel of riches dollar by dollar. Every time you make one of these MONEY KEY transactions, even if you only make a couple dollars on it, you're building your estate.

And doesn't it give you great satisfaction to make those extra dollars simply by knowing how to play the banking game? It's a good feeling to win. Don't you get a special kind of enjoyment out of every penny you earn with the MONEY KEYS? It's like playing Monopoly with real money—and never losing.

Yes, the MONEY KEYS are adding new zest to your living. And the attitude behind them—the attitude of saving, getting the most from your savings, and buying the things you've always wanted with the extra money you make from your savings while you're watching your estate grow—is helping you lead a better life.

But can you lead an *even better* life?

YES, YOU *CAN!*

I'd like to tell you about it in the next section.

Live a life that's
better than the "good" life

Good, better, best,
Never let it rest,
Until good becomes better
And better becomes best.

I have a friend whom I shall call Joe Nameless—not Joe Namath, but Joe Nameless. This Joe is blessed in many respects. He's well educated; he's highly intelligent. Naturally, he has a high-income earning ability.

A sensitive personality, he has been able—because of his good income—to develop many of his sensitivities to a high degree. His taste buds have become so refined that there are barely a handful of restaurants in the city of New York that he classes as good. The average middle- or high-priced restaurant in New York is, according to his standards, not passable; the food, he claims, is practically inedible. He has developed sensitivities in wines and liquors also. Beefeater's or Bellow's or Gilbey's gin is just not acceptable; the gin he drinks has to be some special kind none of us ever heard of. The same goes for every wine and every champagne, scotch, or cognac that passes his lips.

I am trying to paint a picture of Joe because he is a very real and very dear individual to me. Sometimes, in the past, I looked at him and saw him as a very fortunate individual. He has the intellectual tools—as well as the artistic equipment—and he's used his tools and equipment so that, throughout his life, he's been able to live the "good" life. I've gotten to know Joe very well and, by my standards and yours, he *does* live the "good" life. But as I've gotten to know him, I've also realized that there are two problems with the way Joe lives.

One problem is this: Because his standards are so high, almost nothing pleases him. It is very, very rare indeed that he is able to leave a restaurant and say, "That was a good meal. I enjoyed it." It's seldom that he is able to leave a cocktail lounge and say, "The drinks were wonderful." He scarcely ever sips wines and approves of them. His meals are elaborate; but most of his meals he doesn't enjoy at all.

So, in effect, this highly trained gourmet really gets very little pleasure out of drinking or eating. I think of it as being spoiled. He's been spoiled by having too many of the good things; the good things have become commonplace, and only the rare things have become desirable.

It's the same story with his clothes. By getting so accustomed to the good things, only the superb things satisfy him. A $235 or $335 suit, which could make most men happy, doesn't give him the slightest joy, because all his everyday suits fall into that category.

Before I go into Joe Nameless's second problem, let's switch to John Doe, who all his life has had very little. He works to live, and whatever he earns he uses to acquire the minimum necessities of life. John Doe may be in debt or he may be solvent, but he certainly has *not* become accustomed to the "good" things of life.

Let's compare John Doe to Joe Nameless when it comes to eating. When John Doe goes for a meal in a restaurant, the anticipation of that meal—even if the eating place is MacDonald's or the Automat—sets his salivary glands going. Joe Nameless might scorn John Doe's enjoyment of the common hot dog, but John Doe enjoys that common hot dog much more than Joe Nameless enjoys a French meal in what most people would consider a fine French restaurant but which Joe sneers at as third rate.

When John Doe needs a suit, he shops from place to place; and he might spend weeks or months before he buys that suit. But when he *does* buy it—and spends only $29 for it—he gets more enjoyment out of it than Joe Nameless gets out of his $229 suit.

John Doe. Joe Nameless. One man finds life exciting because the commonplace is wonderful; that's John Doe. And it's great to be John Doe. But the other man, Joe Nameless? He's almost pathetic because he has enjoyed so much of life that the wonderful has become commonplace, and it takes the ultimate—the almost unobtainable—to give him enjoyment. His life brings to mind the story of George Sanders, the movie star, who was so successful and had so much of everything that he left a suicide note which explained, "I was bored."

Now let's take a further look at John Doe and Joe Nameless, and you'll understand Joe Nameless's second problem—a problem John Doe doesn't have.

Should anything go wrong financially during John Doe's life, he won't starve to death; he won't freeze because of lack of clothing. That's because when something does go wrong, our society provides him with the necessities of life and John Doe can continue to live without a worry—on much the same scale that he has always lived on. John Doe will not suffer too much when the dollars stop coming in.

But poor, pathetic Joe Nameless! He's got a problem if something should go wrong financially in his life. Despite his high earning capacity, that *could* happen to him. There's an old saying from the days when dollars were coined from silver and were round: "The dollar is round and rolls—sometimes *to* a person, and sometimes *away* from a person." To all of us, no matter how fortunate we are, no matter how steady our high-income earning capacity, there could come a time, as during the 1970–71 recession, when our income is cut down. Joe Nameless is no exception to that rule. And if something does go wrong—unless he has the kind of estate that will permit him to continue to enjoy his "ultimate" type of life-style, and he probably hasn't—Joe Nameless, unlike John Doe, *will* suffer. Because Joe Nameless has become so used to the finest of things, settling for anything less than the best would become a catastrophe.

All you have to do to convince yourself that what I'm saying is true is to look back at the Great Depression which started in 1929. When the stock market crashed, it wasn't the ordinary people, the John Does of our society, who jumped off the roof or put revolvers to their temples and pulled the triggers; it was the people who were making fortunes when the market was climbing. Those were the people who were living high off the hog, who had very high standards; and they couldn't bear to live without all the expensive things to which they had become addicted.

I think we can pick up several guidelines from this story about *poor* Joe Nameless and *rich* John Doe. This is the first guideline:

Whatever our scale of living, we must build an estate that will permit us to continue living on that scale for a year or more. That estate is, so to speak, your insurance fund—because during your lifetime, some catastrophe is likely to strike. You may become ill. You may have an accident. You may be hit by a recession or a depression that shrinks your income. Even if you're a professional man or woman, unless you have an estate that will take care of not just your living but your living on the scale to which you have become accustomed, you stand the risk of being shattered by any financial catastrophe that may strike.

This doesn't mean that in order to build your estate you have to live like a miser. I think I can show you how to build your estate—your *self*-insurance against catastrophe—and lead not the "good" life but a great life. That's the next guideline:

Keep your regular weekly and monthly budget on the conservative side. Watch your pennies very, very carefully. But —whenever you feel you can afford it or need it, go on a *one-shot* splurge. Splurge on an expensive vacation, a very occasional big night on the town, an ultrafancy car (or just a new car for that matter), and so on. When catastrophe strikes, you can forego these *one-shot* splurges *as long as your general scale of living remains the same.*

It's the general scale of living that's important to you, not the occasional splurges. If you have to leave your home and find a smaller apartment, if you have to start eating cheaper food, if you have to clothe yourself less fashionably than you had been doing—if any of your normal living patterns have to be changed, the shocks to you will be far greater than the shocks of foregoing or delaying a one-shot splurge. One-shot splurges can be eliminated should the necessity arise, and they won't be missed much; but lowering your whole scale of living could be a disastrous experience.

So I think that this is a very important guideline for all of us: Hold down your general living scale and use what you consider your excess money—money you can freely spend—for the occasional big splurge.

Joe Nameless insists on having all the "good" things of life and is willing to pay a price for them—a price which is higher than he thinks. But how about you? Why do you often behave like Joe Nameless even though you may not have his big income? Why—when it's so highly desirable to maintain a conservative, regular pattern of living—do you frequently live beyond your means and fail to build the necessary estate that's so important to you when things go wrong?

I've said this many times before, and I want to say it again: It's because you're pushed into the belief that certain things are *the* things to do—*whether you like them or not*. And most often you *don't* like them. But you do them anyway—at great cost to yourself and to your future.

A good many people, seeing an article in the *Sunday Times Magazine* about an elegant French restaurant in New York, will feel compelled to go to that restaurant. Not that they'll enjoy or appreciate the *haute cuisine* or even know what the heck they're ordering. You know what dinner for two costs at that restaurant? Nearly $100! But people go because they've been told that it's *the* thing to do. The same goes for the theater, opera, concerts; for much of the clothes they wear; and for the hairdos they get, whether they're male or female. These people are *fooled* into believing that this is what they enjoy. I'm reminded of the true story of the man who dipped a donkey's tail into paint, held up a canvas as the donkey switched his tail, put the canvas into a frame, and then entered the donkey's painting in a modern art contest. The painting won first prize. A lot of people stood before that jackass's canvas and cried out, "What genius!" Too many people are constantly told that something is *the* thing—that something is good, that something is delicious, that something is worthwhile, that something is beautiful—and they're ashamed to admit that they don't agree.

How about all these people who, having read rave reviews of a play, go to see it—only to find that they don't understand it. Yet they come out of the theater talking about what a wonderful play it was! Look how many people buy expensive subscriptions to the opera—or even more expensive opera tickets from scalpers—and really hate opera. These people are tortured every minute they're in the opera house, but they go and they pretend to enjoy it—simply because they think that it's *the* thing to do.

What you think is *the* thing to do is too often the *wrong* thing to do. You waste more of your income doing what's considered to be *the* thing than in any other way I can think of. You spend your hard-earned dollars for things you don't need, don't want, and don't like. Doing *the* thing is the greatest danger you face when you try to build an estate. Don't you think you should get rid of that danger?

Here's the guideline for doing just that: Don't let yourself fall prey to the phoniness of life. If you enjoy *All in the Family,* watch it on television instead of going to a Metropolitan Opera production of *Die Meistersinger,* which you dislike. Going to the opera, if you *really* don't like it, is not only a waste of money, it's a waste of your valuable time. Be truthful with yourself. Then you'll get two benefits: You'll do the things and buy the things that *truly* make you happy. And you'll save so much money that you'll be able to build your estate faster than you ever thought possible.

What will your friends say about your new life-style of being truthful about your likes and dislikes? You'll quickly find that your friends will agree with you. They'd like to speak up as you do, but they're ashamed to do so. You'll gain new respect. You'll achieve a new status. Over the years, I have spoken up against many sacred cows and I found the people on my side. That was because I was speaking *for* the people, as I continue to do.

Everything I've just told you comes down to this: *You* can be a Joe Nameless if you let yourself be influenced. Instead, build up your estate, keep down your general scale of living, enjoy life more fully with one-time splurges. See through the phoniness of life, and life will give you back happiness, money, and prestige. You'll live a life that's better than the "good" life.

Charge! and watch your
credit cards make money for you

We were just talking about living better. Now I'm going to tell you about a way of living better that will come as a shock to you because you can guess how I feel about going into debt. The way I want to introduce you to is the credit card way.

Let's take a realistic look at the credit card:

The credit card, like dynamite, is a dangerous yet highly useful tool.

With the credit card, you can destroy whatever security you have, whatever estate you may have built up. You can put yourself onto a treadmill of endless and continuing debt. You can bring yourself to the edge of or into bankruptcy.

But properly used, the credit card helps you not only to live better but also to live cheaper, to earn more, and to build your estate and make it grow.

Few people know about these astonishing advantages built into credit cards. With the MONEY KEYS that follow, you'll be able to take advantage of these advantages.

TOP SECRET

Money Key No. 22

How to earn money
on money you've already spent

The advantage:

All the popular credit cards, the bank-issued credit cards like Master Charge and BankAmericard, for instance, give a certain amount of credit *without cost* for a certain period of time. (After that period is up, interest is charged.) Let's see just how long this cost-free credit period is.

Credit card services bill their customers once a month. Its really not a bill you receive; it's a statement for all charges made during the preceding month. The date on which you're billed, your billing date, can be any day of the month. Each card issued has its own billing date. That's because every credit card service spreads its billing dates across the month so that bookkeeping and clerical work can be performed daily, avoiding a jam at the end of the month. So *if you buy merchandise with your credit card today, you have an interest-free period until your billing date.*

Example: If your billing date is the thirtieth and you make your purchase on the first, you get 29 days of free credit.

If your charge is paid within 25 days after the billing date, those 25 days are free as well.

So it's easy to pile up as many as 54 (29 plus 25) cost-free credit days.

How to use this advantage to make money:

The ability to receive this free credit may seem at first glance to be almost meaningless. Why not pay cash if you have the money? But this free credit gives you the opportunity to earn interest on money which you have already spent.

Take this example:

Suppose you buy a refrigerator for $300. If you pay cash for that refrigerator, the $300 comes out of your interest-bearing account. Or if you cash your paycheck to come up with the $300, that $300 could have gone into your interest-bearing account. So, one way or another, paying cash keeps your money from earning interest.

But if you don't pay cash and you charge the cost of the refrigerator on your credit card, you can have nearly two months (54 days) to pay at no cost to you—and for all that time, *the $300 that you've already spent can be earning money in your savings account.*

You can use this MONEY KEY with almost any kind of purchase. Credit cards have become so popular that they can be used in more than a million outlets across the country for all types of goods and services.

I have heard some people say, "Oh, why bother—what I make this way is only $10, $20, or $30 a year." Overcome that stick-in-the-mud attitude. Remember: It's that $10, $20, or $30 per year that makes your estate grow, not shrink. And what you make and save is compounded every year of your life!

TOP SECRET
Money Key No. 23

How to earn **more** money
on money you've already spent

The advantage:

In addition to bank cards and T&E cards (T&E stands for travel and entertainment; cards like American Express are T&E cards), there are oil company travel cards (which are accepted in many places besides gasoline stations) as well as department store, chain store, and mail order credit cards.

A fact that not too many people know is that there isn't a single Master Charge or BankAmericard. Each bank offering either of these cards issues its own version of the card. So you can have Bank A's Master Charge, Bank B's Master Charge, Bank C's Master Charge, and so on. Likewise, you can have Bank D's BankAmericard, Bank E's BankAmericard, Bank F's BankAmericard, and so on.

But a fact known by even fewer people is this: You're not limited to one BankAmericard or one Master Charge card. You can hold as many BankAmericards or Master Charge cards as there are banks near you issuing those cards. Many people hold several Master Charge cards or several BankAmericards or several of each.

What it all adds up to is this: You can carry a great many

103

credit cards. There's a big advantage in doing so.

How to use this advantage to make more money:

In the previous MONEY KEY, you saw how the credit card can give you almost two months of free credit or two months in which the money that you have actually spent can continue to earn interest for you. Now let's see how you can combine that advantage with the advantage of holding many cards to make *more* money.

Let's take the example of the wage earner who would ordinarily cash his paycheck and pay cash for his purchases. Let's assume his weekly spending amounts to $150.

Instead of spending the cash, he charges $150 on his credit card. He has a wallet full of credit cards, all with different billing dates, and the card he uses has the furthest possible billing date: almost a month away. He takes that $150, which he has already spent, and puts it into a day of deposit to day of withdrawal account. Remember, he is not going to have to pay that $150 for almost two months; and for two months he'll be earning interest on that money.

The next week he selects another of his cards that gives him a billing date about a month away and charges his $150 worth of purchases with *that* card. He deposits the $150 and now has $300 in his bank account, drawing interest.

He repeats this procedure week in and week out, always using the credit card with the billing date furthest away from the date of purchase.

Before his first $150 payment becomes due, he finds he's added over $1,400 to his savings account. Moreover, at the time he pays out the $150, he's also depositing another $150 from his paycheck. So, as he continues to use his credit cards and make deposits each week over the course of a year, he builds up an *extra* average balance in his savings account of $1,400.

He has his money in a savings and loan association or a

savings bank. At the interest rate of 5% compounded continuously, giving a yield of 5.20%, he earns approximately $73 in a year.

That $73 is certainly nothing to be sneezed at. In addition, by using credit cards, he gains the convenience of a consolidated bill; and since he no longer has to carry cash around in his pockets, he eliminates the chance of having his money stolen.

TOP SECRET

Money Key No. 24

How to get an extra week's vacation pay

The advantage:

In the last MONEY KEY, you found out how to use credit cards to keep a steady balance of an extra sizable sum of money in your day of deposit to day of withdrawal account.

How to use this advantage to make money:

Once you've built up this kind of steady balance, take the major portion of it and put it into a two-year savings certificate at a nominal rate of 6%, which continuously compounded yields 6.27%. Assuming that your average balance resulting from credit card use is $1,400, that would bring your earnings up to almost $88 per year. (Remember that $1,400 in a day of deposit to day of withdrawal account earns only about $73 a year.)

If you go one step further up the money ladder and use that $1,400 in accordance with the MONEY KEYS in this book, you could easily average 10% on that money during the year. That would give you something like $140. And that's the equivalent of an extra week's vacation pay.

TOP SECRET
Money Key No. 25

How to cut interest charges on your credit card purchases by 33.33%

First, a warning. I do not recommend buying things on credit and then paying off in installments with interest. That's going into debt. That isn't the way to build an estate. The only time I advise going into debt in this fashion is when you can turn your debt into profit (See MONEY KEY No. 32). But in most of our lives the day comes when, to buy what we want when we want it, it's necessary to pay off slowly and with interest. When that day arrives, it's nice to know that there are two ways to slash the cost of that interest. Those ways are described in this MONEY KEY and the next.

The advantage:

Cash advances are available on credit cards. In the state of New York and some other states, the maximum interest that may be charged on cash advances is 12%.

How to use this advantage to save money:

If your credit charges on merchandise or services aren't paid by the payment date—that's 25 days after the billing date—you're usually charged interest at the rate of 18% per year in New York and other states.

The wisest thing to do—if you don't have the cash to pay and you're employing the credit card as a true credit tool—is to draw a cash advance (charging it with any other credit card offering cash advances). Then use that cash advance to pay off what you owe the credit card service for merchandise or services. Pay off on payment day just before interest starts. That wipes out the debt on which you would have to pay 18% and replaces it with a debt on which you have to pay only 12%. You save 33.33% on your credit card interest charges. (This MONEY KEY is not applicable in states like New Jersey which limit interest rates on both charges and cash advances to 12%.)

TOP SECRET

Money Key No. 26

How to cut interest charges on your credit card
purchases by about 50%

The advantage:

You're aware that, in combination with checking accounts,
many banks offer a cash reserve. A cash reserve (the service
was popularized by Chase Manhattan Bank) means you can
write a check even though you don't have the money in your
account to cover it. When such a check comes to your bank
to clear (that is, to be paid from the money in your account),
your bank advances the cash to make your check good. You're
charged interest on the money advanced. Cash reserve is most
effectively and economically used to cover checks that must be
drawn against insufficient funds when your intent is to repay
in full within a few days.

A typical cash reserve interest charge is 12% per year,
the same as the charge on cash advances discussed in the previous MONEY KEY. You can pay your credit card bill with your
cash reserve, just as you did with a cash advance, and cut your
credit card cost by 33.33% (from 18 to 12%). Some banks
charge less for cash reserve than for credit card advances. For
example, Wyoming National Bank's charge for its version of
cash reserve, the "Yes Check," is only 10%.

Cash reserve is your key to cutting credit card cost even further. Since your credit has already been checked for cash reserve, you should be able to obtain a personal loan without delay. Interest rates on personal loans vary with the money markets. The rates charged at this time among a number of banks checked range between 8.5 and 10%, with 9% a good average figure—just half the rate that you have to pay in credit card interest charges.

How to use this advantage to make money:

On your payment date, pay off your credit card charges in full by obtaining a personal loan from the bank in which you have your checking account with cash reserve. Instead of paying 18% on your credit card purchases, you pay the personal loan interest of only about 9%. You cut your credit card interest cost by about 50%.

DANGER!
Money Key No. 27

Traveler's checks cost you more than you think

Traveler's checks offer safety. People have become accustomed to carrying traveler's checks with them when they go on vacations or when they travel for business. But few people realize how dearly they pay for those checks.

Most traveler's checks cost at least $1 per $100. Everybody knows about that. But what few people know is this: There's a *hidden* cost. Let me explain it to you:

You buy your traveler's checks well in advance of the time you use them. So money that could be earning money for you in your savings account doesn't. You lose. But the bank issuing your traveler's checks *is* using *your* money all the time you're *not using* your traveler's checks. And *you* are *paying* the bank for *your* money! You're a two-time loser.

Are you better off when you buy your traveler's checks in spring sales? In those sales, the banks offer any number of traveler's checks in amounts up to $5,000 in return for some small fee like $2 provided you buy your checks in the spring.

Why do banks do this? Bankers know that the vast majority of people won't use the traveler's checks they purchase in spring until summer. What the banks are doing is taking your money in the spring and earning interest on it until your traveler's checks come back to the banks for payment months later.

This is a fine way for banks to make money. But consider: If you keep your money in a savings account and earn the daily interest on it until the time you really need traveler's checks, *you, not* the banks, will make money from spring through summer. Who would you rather have making money on your money—you or the banks?

Traveler's checks bought in spring sales can be among the most expensive bargains you ever bought.

TOP SECRET
Money Key No. 28

How to get free traveler's checks

The advantage:

Barclay's Bank. It's a British based worldwide bank larger than any bank in this country. It's a banking empire with branches in more than a hundred countries, including countries many of us have never heard of. Barclay's traveler's checks are honored everywhere.

How to use this advantage to save money:

Why is Barclay's an advantage? Because this bank will happily issue all the traveler's checks you want at no charge to you. All you pay is the face amount of the checks. You don't pay $2 a hundred or $1 a hundred or any commission or fee of any kind. Barclay's traveler's checks are *really* free!

Barclay's has three branches in New York, including one at Kennedy International Airport, plus two branches in Chicago and thirty-two in California. Even though it's a British bank, Barclay's automatically issues its traveler's checks in dollars in its American branches; but you can get Barclay's traveler's checks in any of the world's currencies.

Barclay's will not send their traveler's checks to you

through the mail. You have to get them in person at one of the bank's branch offices. But if you're not near a Barclay's branch and you're traveling to Europe by plane, you can stop off at Kennedy Airport and buy your free traveler's checks at the Barclay's branch there. Certified and teller's checks are accepted.

Warning: Free traveler's checks really aren't free. You buy them with money that was in or could have gone into your savings account. The moment you use that money for traveler's checks, that money ceases to earn interest for you. In the following MONEY KEYS, I'll tell you how you can avoid this drain on your interest—and still travel with safety.

TOP SECRET

Money Key No. 29

How to earn money
while you're enjoying yourself on a vacation
—without working

The advantages:

Your credit card is virtually as safe as a traveler's check thanks to the recent federal law limiting your liability when you lose your credit card and somebody fraudulently runs up charges on it.

Of course, if your credit cards are stolen or lost while you're traveling, they aren't easily replaced, and that's an inconvenience. But you're not that much better off when you lose your traveler's checks. It isn't as easy getting your money back as the advertisements make it sound. You can go through a lot of trouble before you get the money you need to continue your vacation.

Another advantage of the better-known credit cards is that they're accepted almost everywhere. I told you in the previous MONEY KEY that Barclay's Bank is known even in the remotest countries of the world. So is Barclay's credit card. Barclay's has a reciprocal agreement with BankAmericard; wherever Barclay's credit card is acceptable, BankAmericard is acceptable. BankAmericards and Barclay's credit cards are like instant money all over the world.

True, if you stop along the road in a foreign country, the proprietor of some little restaurant might not honor your Bank-Americard or Master Charge. But he might not take your traveler's check either. And, by the by, did you ever try to pay with traveler's checks in the smaller shops and restaurants in New York City? It's not easy. But almost every retail store and eating place will accept one credit card or another.

How to use these advantages to make money:

Instead of buying traveler's checks, use your credit cards. Your money *stays* in your savings account and keeps earning money.

Moreover, when you use your credit cards away from home, it takes longer until you're billed. You may be billed two or three months later than you would be billed if you had made the credit card purchases back home. You get *extra* free credit time—and that's more time for your money in the bank to earn *extra* money.

Money Key No. 30

Another way to earn money
while you're enjoying yourself on a vacation
—still without working

I've shown you that investing in traveler's checks, even in free traveler's checks, means a sizable loss to you in interest. In the last MONEY KEY I've shown you how to use credit cards instead of traveler's checks to make money on your vacation instead of losing it.

"But," some people ask, "I'd better have some cash with me anyway. So I'll have to buy some traveler's checks for safety's sake, won't I?"

The answer is, you can get along with very little cash or the equivalent in traveler's checks. This MONEY KEY will show you how to spend all the cash you like—without the risk of carrying cash and without the need to carry traveler's checks. Moreover, I'll show you how to *earn money on the cash you spend for many days after you spend it.*

The advantages:

With many checking accounts, banks offer check guarantee cards. These cards guarantee that your check is good. Guarantee cards are recognized all over the world. Your checks plus your guarantee card is the same as cash and as safe as traveler's checks.

But if you use your checks on vacation, you want to be

117

sure that you have enough money in your checking account to cover them. This means that before you leave you have to transfer funds from your savings account to your checking account. Those funds no longer earn interest. You're no better off than if you'd bought free traveler's checks.

To overcome this drawback, add the use of another advantage: No matter where you are—in Europe, Asia, anyplace in the world—it's easy to transfer money from your day of deposit to day of withdrawal account to your checking account.

How to use these advantages to make money:

When you're on vacation, if you can't use your credit cards, use your personal checks and your guarantee card.

No matter how far away you are from home, take advantage of your ability to transfer funds from your savings account to your checking account in one of the following ways:

Keep only a small balance in your checking account. When you find that you need more money, all you do is mail your passbook to your bank with an authorization to transfer some of your money out of your savings account into your checking account.

Or, before you leave, go to the bank officer who handles your account and leave your passbook with him. A letter from you to him will arrange the transfer of funds from your savings account to your checking account as you need it.

Or leave your bank written authorization to withdraw whatever sums are needed from your savings account to cover any check in excess of your checking account balance. Most bankers will gladly follow your instructions. If you're afraid your check will bounce, don't be. A bank doesn't bounce a check on a regular customer. Your check guarantee card further ensures that the bank won't bounce your check. And when you make arrangements with your banker to back up your check with your savings account, you can be absolutely sure your check won't bounce.

Use your guaranteed checks like cash or to get cash. But keep most or all of your funds in a day of deposit to day of with-drawal account. Until your checks come back to the bank, your money will be earning interest. You'll be earning money on the cash you spend for many days after you spend it.

Your checking account and savings account need not be in the same bank. One bank is always happy to take your funds out of another bank. But if both accounts are in the same bank, it makes the transfer of funds simple. When you go on a trip, it might be advisable to keep a savings account in the same bank in which you keep your checking account. Work out the details with your local banker, who should be happy to accom-modate you.

TOP SECRET

Money Key No. 31

How to use your credit card to get discounts

The advantage:

When you charge a purchase with your credit card, it costs *the retailer* about 5 to 7% of that purchase. He has to pay that money to the bank or service that issues your credit card.

How to use this advantage to save money:

I'll give you a simple example.

We were redoing our kitchen and two foyers with a well-known brand of tile. My wife and I went to a large discount chain store and picked out the tiles we liked. We ordered them. We were told they would be delivered from the warehouse. The bill for the tiles ran something like $400. We were informed that any deposit would be all right, and we could pay the balance C.O.D.

I knew, from the decals I had noticed on the storefront as I came in, that the store honored several of the credit cards I carry. I took out one of those cards and held it in my hand.

I said to the salesman, "Yes, I can put down a cash deposit and pay for the balance later. *Or* I can use my credit card. You know, the card offers me an advantage. I don't have to pay for this purchase for quite a while, and my money can go on earning interest in my savings account. But I'm willing to give up that advantage. I won't use my credit card if you give me a discount for cash. In that case I'll pay cash."

The salesman said, "I think something can be arranged. Let me see."

He had already written up the bill, and he took it over to the cashier's desk. The man at the cashier's desk seemed to have the authority to make a decision. The salesman had gone ahead of me, and by the time I caught up with him, the man at the cashier's desk had taken the bill and was holding his pencil over it.

He said, "Suppose we just knock off the sales tax."

For a moment I was flabbergasted, because the sales tax is 7%. This was a sizable discount considering that the store is a large discount operation and I was paying well below the list price of the tiles to begin with.

I said to this man, "How can you afford to give me 7%? I know that the average charge you have to pay on this bank-issued credit card is about 5%. Actually you're losing 2%!"

He answered, "Fact is, we're losing more. We pay less than 5%. We do so much business with the credit card people, and our price tags are so large, that we get charged only 4.5%. But we're happy to give you 7%. Want to know why? We're so disgusted with having to take money off the top—to skim off the cream of our sales—and pay it to the credit card people, that if our customers are willing to pay cash, we'll give them *more* of a savings than the cost of the credit is to us."

The chances are if you show a retailer your credit card and say, "I'll use my credit card or I'll pay cash if you give me a discount," you'll end up with a discount.

The retailer would rather give *you* the 5% than give it to

the bank or credit card service. Some retailers will give you only part of that 5%, and some, like the discount house I told you about, will give you more.

Introducing the noncrime

One of the most interesting results of the widespread use of credit cards is a kind of crime which isn't really a crime at all. I call it "the noncrime."

To understand it, let's start by going back a bit. There was a time when, if you wanted credit, you really had to be deserving of credit. A bank wouldn't give you a loan unless the loan officer was very sure you could and would repay. If your credit rating wasn't good enough, bankers saw to it that you put up collateral; or bankers would approve your loan only if somebody whose credit rating *was* good enough cosigned it. The chance of a bank taking a loss was extremely small. Less than 1/10 of 1% of bank loans went bad.

Then came the bank credit card. In the mid-sixties, banks distributed millions of credit cards by mail to people who never asked for them. Bankers never bothered to check the credit ratings of the people who received their cards. The banking industry was going along on the proved fact that most people paid their debts.

Bankers knew, of course, that there'd be some people who'd be seduced by free credit cards into running up charges they couldn't repay. But the percentage of these people, bankers figured, would be so small that the banks could easily afford to absorb the losses. Events proved the bankers to be right. To-day, just as department stores figure shrinkage in inventories due to shoplifting into their overhead, so banks figure bad cred-it card debts into *their* overhead.

Shoplifting is a real crime. But buying more than one can afford to pay for, providing it's not done with fraudulent in-tent, is not a crime at all. Yet the credit card abuser gets goods and services for which he doesn't pay, and what he's doing is not morally right. It's a kind of crime which isn't really a crime —a noncrime. The credit card deadbeat is a noncriminal.

Banks can't prosecute a noncriminal. They try to collect, of course. But remember, the loss from credit card bad debts is figured into their overhead. That loss is passed on to the con-sumer and retailer in the cost of credit. So if the banks don't collect, they don't really lose anything. That explains the at-titude of bankers toward credit card noncriminals, which is, "If they won't pay or can't pay, we'll just forget about it."

Some interesting stories concerning this noncrime have come to my attention. There's one story that tickles me, and I think you might get a smile from it as well—and maybe a tear.

I'll refer to the old man in this story as Gramps, because that's just what he was, a Grandpa. All through his life, he had worked to support his large family of children. The children grew up and had large families of their own. Still Gramps con-tinued to work. He didn't earn very much. He lived modestly.

Several years ago he was showered with what seemed to him like manna from heaven. He received several free credit cards in the mail. He began to use them from time to time be-cause of their convenience. That gave him a taste for credit cards. Gradually, he collected all kinds of credit cards until he had a large stack of them.

He used all his credit cards at one time or another. He al-

ways paid his bills. He always paid by the due date. Last year
—when this happened—Gramps was more than ninety years
old; but even though Gramps was living on his Social Security
benefits, his credit cards had never been revoked. He was free
to use one or all of them.

Christmas came. He thought of his large family—dozens
of children, grandchildren, and even great-grandchildren. He
thought of the Christmases of the past when all he was able
to give his family were little things or nothing at all. And here
he was, over ninety, with not much time left. Sorrowfully he
asked himself, "Will I ever be able to do anything wonderful
for the family I love so much?" Then something snapped. He
had credit cards, didn't he?" Why not use them? Somehow,
some way, he'd find the money to pay off his debts.

He used his credit cards to buy lovely Christmas gifts for
his children, his grandchildren, and his great-grandchildren.
He bought them toys, hi-fis, stereos, tape recorders, TV sets,
gift certificates—whatever he thought would give them pleasure. He charged airplane tickets to bring his far-flung family
together for the holidays.

Of course, Gramps never found the money to pay his bills.
And the credit card companies and the banks never pressed
him. Gramps's noncrime had already been figured into their
overhead.

It was the happiest Christmas Gramps's family ever had.
It was the happiest Christmas Gramps ever had.

TOP SECRET

Money Key No. 32

How to turn your debts into profits

In another book,* I wrote that credit card buying is addictive, and it can, when misused, lead to much personal suffering. Once you're hooked, you can get into debt way over your head. There are few other situations in everyday life that can make you feel more miserable.

But if you use your credit cards wisely, *you can turn your debts into profits.* YES, YOU *CAN.*

I'd like to tell you about one way I've done it.

Let's assume we're in the month of December. I know that I'm going to need a pair of shoes by March, a few months away. I've often found it cheapest in the long run to buy the best, and that goes for shoes as well as anything else. I look in a shoe store window. I see a model that I like. The price is $42. But I know that in January this store will hold a clearance sale and many shoes will be marked down to about $20.

The model I want is likely to go on sale. New models are coming in, and the store wants to get rid of styles that have

*CREDIT-CARDSMANSHIP: *How to Survive the Credit Card Nightmare and Turn Plastic into Gold,* Martin J. Meyer, Farnsworth Publishing Company, Rockville Centre, New York.

suddenly become "old." What about buying "old"-style shoes when they're on sale? Actually, the new styles aren't that much different. As an example, many new-style shoes are exactly the same as the old-style shoes except for the perforations. Sometimes perforations are added and sometimes perforations are removed. But my feet don't know whether my shoes have perforations or not. If I have a comfortable last in a well-made shoe, my feet are happy. So buying a $42 shoe on sale for $20, even though the style doesn't have all the up-to-the-minute perforations or lack of them, doesn't bother me at all.

But there have been Januarys when I didn't have the extra $20 to spend on a pair of shoes. I could have skipped the sale those times, couldn't I? But I knew that by March I was really going to need those shoes. If I waited until March, those very same shoes which I could buy in January for $20 would cost me more than twice as much. It made sense to buy the shoes in January. But how could I do that without money?

I don't like to use credit on which I have to pay interest. That costs me money. But I saw that here was a case where I could use credit, pay interest, and *make* money. This is what I did:

I used my credit card to charge the pair of shoes I wanted *at the sale price*. No matter how I figured it, the interest charges couldn't raise the price of the shoes more than $2. I got a pair of shoes for $20 plus, let's say, $2 in interest charges—a total of only $22.

Without the use of my credit card, those shoes would have cost me $42 in March. I had put $20 in my pocket.

So you see how debts can really be turned into profits. In a nutshell, this is how it's done:

There are occasions when you will need something in the future that can be bought now at a greatly reduced price. If you can't afford to lay out the cash, buy on credit. Even after adding the cost of the credit, you make a substantial profit. On those shoes I just told you about, I spent less than $2 on interest charges to make $20 for myself. That's a 900% gain, and there's no business in the world that comes close to making that kind of profit.

Get a real bargain every time you buy

In the last MONEY KEY, I talked about sales. Sales are an important source of found money. But be sure that you're really getting a bargain.

You know, when it comes to buying, many people fall into one of two types: those who buy something and boast that it cost more than it did and those who buy something and boast that it cost less than it did. The first type of buyer thinks he's improving his image because people believe he's buying expensive things. The second type of buyer, with his imaginary bargains, thinks he impresses people with his superior ability to buy for less.

Both types may think they're fooling other people, but they're only fooling themselves. Neither type really impresses anyone.

What you really have to do is buy less and buy for less. Then you'll impress *yourself*—the only important person to impress.

And of course, you buy for less at *real* sales—sales that save you money: clearance sales, January sales, July sales, semi-annual sales, white sales, and a thousand and one other kinds of sales. Get used to planning your purchases ahead so that *whenever you buy, you save.* As an example, buy that new bathing suit in the middle of summer and save at least half its May cost. When you plan your purchases this way, you gain the satisfaction of knowing that *you get a real bargain every time you buy.*

Put the money you save into the bank. It will make your estate grow faster. And the more you save, the faster it will grow.

But savings accounts aren't the only *safe* ways to invest your savings. I'd like to tell you about some other ways. But before I get to them, I want to introduce you to a concept you must know about before you can take advantage of these safe nonbanking investments. That concept is your *true* income tax bracket. I don't think more than one person in a thousand knows what his *true* income tax bracket is. If you're not that one person, you'll find out how to figure your true income tax bracket in the next section.

Know your **true** income tax bracket—
it can make the difference
between riches and poverty

Joe Smith is single. He earned $10,000 (adjusted gross income before deductions) in 1971. He paid $1,591 in federal income taxes (using standard deductions). That's almost 16% of his gross income, so Joe Smith assumed he was in the 16% income tax bracket.

He was wrong.

He was in the 25% federal income tax bracket.

He paid 25% on the last $25 he made. He will pay 25% on the next $2,000 he might make.

That means Joe Smith will pay the Internal Revenue Service at least 25 cents out of every additional dollar he'll earn, not 16 cents as he had assumed. His actual federal income tax bracket (25%) was actually more than 50% higher than the bracket (16%) that he thought he was in.

But that still wasn't Joe Smith's *total* income tax bracket.

Joe Smith had to pay state income tax as well. On his income of $10,000, Joe paid New York State $323. Joe figured that amounted to about 3.25%, so he was in the 3.25% state income tax bracket. Joe was wrong again.

Joe paid 6% to the state tax bureau on the last $1,000 of his income and will pay 6% on the next $1,000. His true state tax bracket at 6% was almost twice what he thought it was.

To figure out his federal *plus* state income tax bracket, Joe Smith made the following addition:

Federal tax	$1,591
State tax	323
	$1,914

That total was about 19% of $10,000, and Joe concluded that he was in the 19% bracket. Once again, Joe was wrong.

Remember, Joe was really in the 25% *federal* income tax bracket and the 6% *state* income tax bracket, and 25% plus 6% added up to—not 19%, but—31%!

Joe's true total income tax bracket was even higher, because he lived in New York City and had to pay a city income tax. But, putting city income tax aside (not all cities have it), Joe's *true* income tax bracket, his ITB, of 31% was 63% higher than he had figured it to be.

Joe didn't know how to calculate his true ITB. *You* should know how—if you're serious about becoming rich. Your true ITB can be the crucial factor in decisions that will determine whether your estate will shrink, stagnate, or mushroom.

Here's how you can determine your true federal income tax bracket for *any* year. (I'm using the 1971 tables simply to show you what to do.)

STEP No 1. Find your *taxable* income. You do that by subtracting standard deductions and exemptions from your adjusted gross income. If, for example, you're single and you earn $10,000 a year, here's how your federal taxable income is computed:

Adjusted gross income $10,000
Less standard deduction*   1,300
                                  ────────
                                    8,700
Less exemption (1 person)   675
                                  ────────
                                  $ 8,025

*As your income and tax brackets increase, itemizing deductions is usually more advantageous than taking standard deductions. In computing your ITB on the basis of itemized deductions, take into account that state taxes are deductible from income for federal tax purposes.

STEP No 2. Refer to the relevant federal tax table. If you're single, that table is Schedule X.

FORM 1040
U.S. INDIVIDUAL INCOME TAX RETURN

	Over—	But not over—		of excess over—
1.	$500	$1,000	$70+15%	$500
2.	$1,000	$1,500	$145+16%	$1,000
3.	$1,500	$2,000	$225+17%	$1,500
4.	$2,000	$4,000	$310+19%	$2,000
5.	$4,000	$6,000	$690+21%	$4,000
6.	$6,000	$8,000	$1,110+24%	$6,000
7.	$8,000	$10,000	$1,590+25%	$8,000
8.	$10,000	$12,000	$2,090+27%	$10,000
9.	$12,000	$14,000	$2,630+29%	$12,000
10.	$14,000	$16,000	$3,210+31%	$14,000
11.	$16,000	$18,000	$3,830+34%	$16,000
12.	$18,000	$20,000	$4,510+36%	$18,000
13.	$20,000	$22,000	$5,230+38%	$20,000
14.	$22,000	$26,000	$5,990+40%	$22,000
15.	$26,000	$32,000	$7,590+45%	$26,000
16.	$32,000	$38,000	$10,290+50%	$32,000
17.	$38,000	$44,000	$13,290+55%	$38,000
18.	$44,000	$50,000	$16,590+60%	$44,000
19.	$50,000	$60,000	$20,190+62%	$50,000

Since your taxable income is $8,025, line 7 is applicable to you. According to that line, your tax is $1,590 *plus* 25% of everything over $8,000. On the $25 of your taxable income in excess of $8,000, your federal tax bracket is 25%. Should your income increase by, let's say, $500, that $500 would be subject to a 25% tax. Your true federal income tax bracket is 25%!

Here's another example:

You're single and your adjusted gross income is $15,000.

STEP No. 1. Find your taxable income, as follows:

Adjusted gross income	$15,000
Less standard deduction	1,500
	13,500
Less exemption (1 person)	675
Federal taxable income	$12,825

STEP No. 2. Refer to the relevant federal tax table.

Line 9 of Schedule X shows that your tax is $2,630 plus 29% of everything over $12,000. Your *true* federal income tax bracket is 29%.

To determine your true state income tax bracket, follow the same procedure. Here's how it works out if you're single and earning $10,000 in New York State.

STEP No. 1. Find your *taxable* income, as follows:

Adjusted gross income	$10,000
Less standard deduction	1,300
	8,700
Less exemption (1 person)	650
State taxable income	$ 8,050

STEP No 2. Refer to the relevant state tax table.

IT-201
NEW YORK STATE INCOME TAX RESIDENT RETURN

		Tax Rate Schedule	
	over	but not over	enter on line 10, page 1
1.	$ 0	$1,000	2% of amount on line 9
2.	1,000	3,000	$20 plus 3% of excess over $1,000
3.	3,000	5,000	80 plus 4% " " " 3,000
4.	5,000	7,000	160 plus 5% " " " 5,000
5.	7,000	9,000	260 plus (6%) " " " 7,000
6.	9,000	11,000	380 plus 7% " " " 9,000
7.	11,000	13,000	520 plus 8% " " " 11,000
8.	13,000	15,000	680 plus 9% " " " 13,000
9.	15,000	17,000	860 plus 10% " " " 15,000
10.	17,000	19,000	1,060 plus 11% " " " 17,000
11.	19,000	21,000	1,280 plus 12% " " " 19,000
12.	21,000	23,000	1,520 plus 13% " " " 21,000
13.	23,000		1,780 plus 14% " " " 23,000

Line 5 indicates that you must pay 6 cents out of every dollar earned over $7,000 to the state taxing authorities. Your *true* state income tax bracket is 6%.

To compute your true total income tax bracket, add your true state and federal income tax brackets (plus your true city income tax bracket if applicable).

Here's how high your true ITBs were in 1971 if you were earning $10,000, $15,000 or $20,000 a year. (Computations are made on the basis of standard deductions allowable.)

For Adjusted Gross Income of $10,000

Income tax bracket	Single person (not head of household)	Married persons (filing joint return with number of children)		
		0	1	2
Federal	25%	19%	19%	19%
State	6%	6%	5%	5%
True ITB	31%	25%	24%	24%

For Adjusted Gross Income of $15,000

Income tax bracket	Single person (not head of household)	Married persons (filing joint return with number of children)		
		0	1	2
Federal	29%	25%	22%	22%
State	8%	8%	8%	7%
True ITB	37%	33%	30%	29%

For Adjusted Gross Income of $20,000

Income tax bracket	Single person (not head of household)	Married persons (filing joint return with number of children)		
		0	1	2
Federal	34%	28%	28%	25%
State	11%	11%	10%	10%
True ITB	45%	39%	38%	35%

Take out your tax records today and determine your true ITB. It will be of critical importance to your future.

How to determine the yield you need
to stay ahead of inflation—
and **really** make your estate grow

Now that you've figured out your true ITB, let's put it to work
to determine whether your savings are *really* growing.

In evaluating the real value of your savings, it's the net
yield after taxes that counts, not the interest rate you're paid.
Here's a table that shows you how to determine your net yield
with the aid of your true ITB.

Your True ITB	YOUR NET YIELD AFTER TAXES AT THE NOMINAL INTEREST RATES SHOWN						
	4½%	5%	5½%	6%	7%	8%	9%
20%	3.6	4.0	4.4	4.8	5.6	6.4	7.2
24%	3.4	3.8	4.2	4.6	5.3	6.1	6.8
28%	3.2	3.6	4.0	4.3	5.0	5.8	6.5
32%	3.1	3.4	3.7	4.1	4.8	5.4	6.1
36%	2.9	3.2	3.5	3.9	4.5	5.1	5.7
40%	2.7	3.0	3.3	3.6	4.2	4.8	5.4
44%	2.5	2.8	3.1	3.4	3.9	4.5	5.0
48%	2.3	2.6	2.9	3.1	3.6	4.2	4.6
52%	2.2	2.4	2.7	2.9	3.4	3.8	4.3
56%	2.0	2.2	2.4	2.6	3.1	3.5	4.0
60%	1.8	2.0	2.2	2.4	2.8	3.2	3.6

Example: If your true ITB is 20% (first horizontal line) and you invest your money in a commercial bank at 4.5% (second vertical column), your net yield is 3.6% (meeting of first horizontal line with second vertical column).

Considering the ravages of inflation in recent years, this chart shows you at a glance whether your investments are losing money, holding their own, or making money.

If your net yield after taxes falls in the dark gray area, your savings are dwindling away. Each year your nest egg is worth less than it was the previous year—less in buying power, the only real measure of savings.

If your net yield falls in the light-gray area, the value of your savings is remaining about the same. That means you're being paid *nothing* for giving the banks the use of your money.

It's only if your net yield falls in the white area that you are gaining a true return for the use of your money.

A glance at this chart shows you that if you are in the lower tax brackets, you must get at least 7% in taxable return just to stand still. Higher brackets require a return of 8%, 9%, or more. The chart proves mathematically that when you put your money in a bank at 4.5, 5, or even 6%, you're really losing.

Investments as safe as savings accounts
—and they pay more

Now that you know what yield you need to make your estate grow and you know that you can't get that yield just by putting your money in savings accounts at the advertised rates, the next question is: How do you get the yield you need *safely?*

One way, of course, is to use the MONEY KEYS in this book which show you how to multiply the advertised interest rates on your savings. But using these MONEY KEYS requires a certain amount of activity—making transactions, running back and forth to the bank—and there are some people who can't go to this trouble and other people who prefer not to. These people will find they're better off putting their money in investments other than savings accounts.

"But how can we be sure our money is safe?" these people ask. "At least our money is federally insured when we invest it in a savings account. We can't lose our principal as we could with other investments."

These people, like most savings account depositors, overestimate the safety value of "federal" insurance. It's *not* "federal" insurance, it's federal *agency* insurance. Your savings account insurance is *not* backed by the faith and credit of the United States government. It's backed only by the federal insuring agency's own assets—and those assets are pitifully small.

Even the Comptroller General of the United States warned the Congress of a potential federal agency insurance disaster. In the event that more than a handful of banks were to fail at the same time, he said, the insurance money in the federal agency treasury would be wiped out. Your savings account money could be insured up to $20,000 and, in case your bank failed, you might not see a penny of your money again.

Keep in mind a point I've made over and over again: Putting money in the bank at advertised rates is not only really gambling, but gambling on a sure loser. So stop playing safe—and losing. Particularly when what you're doing is not all that safe.

That doesn't mean you're to throw caution to the winds and rush into speculation. You're not a gambler. Your goal is the preservation and building of your savings. You don't want to stake all you've built up over a lifetime in the hope of a big gain. It's too risky. If, instead of settling for the slow and steady loss you get from banks, you decide to speculate, gamble deliberately, you can be wiped out clean—and fast. You must avoid the "get-rich-quick" investments such as:

- Stocks—common and preferred
- Stock warrants and rights
- Convertible bonds (corporate)
- Real estate—syndications and individual
- Mutual funds (at least 99.44% of them)
- Lotteries and sweepstakes
- Gambling casinos

You must remain conservative and stick to safe investments—investments that will not only earn enough to offset inflation's shrinking effect on the value of your dollar but also pay you something in addition to compensate you for the use of your money. There are many such investments which are just

about as safe as or even safer than bank accounts. Investments
of this type include, from time to time, the following:

- Treasury bills
- Government bonds
- U.S. government agency bonds
- Municipal bonds—high grade (tax-exempt)
- Corporate bonds—high grade (debentures)
- Mutual funds that invest exclusively in U.S.
  government securities
- Municipal bond trusts

Municipal bonds are currently enjoying great popularity
—mainly because of their tax-exempt feature. Income earned
from these bonds is exempt from taxation. Corporate bonds are
taxable, but they pay higher yields than municipals. Which
should you invest in—the higher-yield but taxable corporate
bonds, or the lower-yield but tax-exempt municipal bonds? The
answer depends on your ITB, as you can see when you examine
the two tables I've made up for you.

Table I shows your after-tax, or tax-exempt, yields for true
ITBs of from 15 to 57% for taxable yields of from 4 to 15%.

Example: If you earn a taxable yield of 7% (see arrow
pointing horizontally) and your true ITB is 25% (see arrow
pointing vertically), your after-tax yield is 5.25%. In other
words, for a true ITB of 25%, a 7% taxable yield is equivalent
to a 5.25% tax-exempt yield.

TABLE I
AFTER-TAX OR TAX-EXEMPT YIELDS (PERCENT) FOR TRUE INCOME TAX BRACKETS OF

Taxable yield (annual)	15%	17%	19%	21%	23%	25%	27%	30%	33%	36%	39%	42%	45%	49%	53%	57%
15.00	12.75	12.45	12.15	11.85	11.55	11.25	10.95	10.50	10.05	9.60	9.15	8.70	8.25	7.65	7.05	6.45
14.50	12.33	12.04	11.75	11.46	11.17	10.88	10.59	10.15	9.72	9.28	8.85	8.41	7.98	7.40	6.82	6.24
14.00	11.90	11.62	11.34	11.06	10.78	10.50	10.22	9.80	9.38	8.96	8.54	8.12	7.70	7.14	6.58	6.02
13.50	11.48	11.21	10.94	10.67	10.40	10.13	9.86	9.45	9.05	8.64	8.24	7.83	7.43	6.89	6.35	5.81
13.00	11.05	10.79	10.53	10.27	10.01	9.75	9.49	9.10	8.71	8.32	7.93	7.54	7.15	6.63	6.11	5.59
12.50	10.63	10.38	10.13	9.88	9.63	9.38	9.13	8.75	8.38	8.00	7.63	7.25	6.88	6.38	5.88	5.38
12.00	10.20	9.96	9.72	9.48	9.24	9.00	8.76	8.40	8.04	7.68	7.32	6.96	6.60	6.12	5.64	5.16
11.50	9.78	9.55	9.32	9.09	8.86	8.63	8.40	8.05	7.71	7.36	7.02	6.67	6.33	5.87	5.41	4.95
11.00	9.35	9.13	8.91	8.69	8.47	8.25	8.03	7.70	7.37	7.04	6.71	6.38	6.05	5.61	5.17	4.73
10.50	8.93	8.72	8.51	8.30	8.09	7.88	7.67	7.35	7.04	6.72	6.41	6.09	5.78	5.36	4.94	4.52
10.00	8.50	8.30	8.10	7.90	7.70	7.50	7.30	7.00	6.70	6.40	6.10	5.80	5.50	5.10	4.70	4.30
9.50	8.08	7.89	7.70	7.51	7.32	7.13	6.94	6.65	6.37	6.08	5.80	5.51	5.23	4.85	4.47	4.09
9.00	7.65	7.47	7.29	7.11	6.93	6.75	6.57	6.30	6.03	5.76	5.49	5.22	4.95	4.59	4.23	3.87
8.50	7.23	7.06	6.89	6.72	6.55	6.38	6.21	5.95	5.70	5.44	5.19	4.93	4.68	4.34	4.00	3.66
8.00	6.80	6.64	6.48	6.32	6.16	6.00	5.84	5.60	5.36	5.12	4.88	4.64	4.40	4.08	3.76	3.44
7.50	6.38	6.23	6.08	5.93	5.78	5.63	5.48	5.25	5.03	4.80	4.58	4.35	4.13	3.83	3.53	3.23
7.00	5.95	5.81	5.67	5.53	5.39	(5.25)	5.11	4.90	4.69	4.48	4.27	4.06	3.85	3.57	3.29	3.01
6.50	5.53	5.40	5.27	5.14	5.01	4.88	4.75	4.55	4.36	4.16	3.97	3.77	3.58	3.32	3.06	2.80
6.00	5.10	4.98	4.86	4.74	4.62	4.50	4.38	4.20	4.02	3.84	3.66	3.48	3.30	3.06	2.82	2.58
5.50	4.68	4.57	4.46	4.35	4.24	4.13	4.02	3.85	3.69	3.52	3.36	3.19	3.03	2.81	2.59	2.37
5.00	4.25	4.15	4.05	3.95	3.85	3.75	3.65	3.50	3.35	3.20	3.05	2.90	2.75	2.55	2.35	2.15
4.50	3.83	3.74	3.65	3.56	3.47	3.38	3.29	3.15	3.02	2.88	2.75	2.61	2.48	2.30	2.12	1.94
4.00	3.40	3.32	3.24	3.16	3.08	3.00	2.92	2.80	2.68	2.56	2.44	2.32	2.20	2.04	1.88	1.72

Table II shows equivalent taxable yields for true ITBs of from 15 to 57% for tax-exempt, or after-tax, yields of from 2 to 9%.

Example: If a municipal bond offers you a 5% tax-exempt yield (see arrow pointing horizontally) and your ITB is 36% (see arrow pointing vertically), you would have to earn 7.81% taxable to equal the 5% nontaxable.

Using these tables, you can decide on the basis of your true ITB whether to invest in taxable bonds or nontaxable municipals.

Example: If your true ITB is 25% and you have a choice between a taxable corporate bond at 7% or a nontaxable municipal at 4.75%, it's obvious from the example I gave you using Table I that you're better off with the taxable 7% bond, since you need a nontaxable yield of 5.25% (not 4.75%) to equal the 7% bond.

Another example: If your true ITB is 36% and you have a choice between a tax-exempt municipal at 5% and a taxable corporate bond at 7%, it's clear from the example I gave you using Table II that you're better off with the municipal bond, since you would need a taxable yield of 7.81% (not 7%) to equal the 5% bond.

Here's a rule of thumb concerning the selection of a tax-exempt municipal as against a taxable bond: the higher your ITB, the more attractive low but tax-exempt yields become.

TABLE II

EQUIVALENT TAXABLE YIELDS (PERCENT) FOR TRUE INCOME TAX BRACKETS OF

Tax-exempt yields (annual)	15%	17%	19%	21%	23%	25%	27%	30%	33%	36%	39%	42%	45%	49%	53%	57%
2.00	2.35	2.41	2.47	2.53	2.60	2.67	2.74	2.86	2.99	3.13	3.28	3.45	3.64	3.92	4.34	4.65
2.25	2.65	2.71	2.78	2.85	2.92	3.00	3.08	3.21	3.36	3.52	3.69	3.88	4.09	4.41	4.88	5.23
2.50	2.94	3.01	3.09	3.16	3.25	3.33	3.42	3.57	3.73	3.91	4.10	4.31	4.55	4.90	5.43	5.81
2.75	3.24	3.31	3.39	3.48	3.57	3.67	3.77	3.93	4.10	4.30	4.51	4.74	5.00	5.39	5.97	6.40
3.00	3.53	3.61	3.70	3.80	3.90	4.00	4.11	4.29	4.48	4.69	4.92	5.17	5.45	5.88	6.51	6.98
3.25	3.82	3.92	4.01	4.11	4.22	4.33	4.45	4.64	4.85	5.08	5.33	5.60	5.91	6.37	7.05	7.56
3.50	4.12	4.22	4.32	4.43	4.55	4.67	4.79	5.00	5.22	5.47	5.74	6.03	6.36	6.86	7.60	8.14
3.75	4.41	4.52	4.63	4.75	4.87	5.00	5.14	5.36	5.60	5.86	6.15	6.47	6.82	7.35	8.14	8.72
4.00	4.71	4.82	4.94	5.06	5.19	5.33	5.48	5.71	5.97	6.25	6.56	6.90	7.27	7.84	8.68	9.30
4.25	5.00	5.12	5.25	5.38	5.52	5.67	5.82	6.07	6.34	6.64	6.97	7.33	7.73	8.33	9.22	9.88
4.50	5.29	5.42	5.56	5.70	5.84	6.00	6.16	6.43	6.72	7.03	7.38	7.76	8.18	8.82	9.77	10.47
4.75	5.59	5.72	5.86	6.01	6.17	6.33	6.51	6.79	7.09	7.42	7.79	8.19	8.64	9.31	10.31	11.05
5.00	5.88	6.02	6.17	6.33	6.49	6.67	6.85	7.14	7.46	(7.81)	8.20	8.62	9.09	9.80	10.85	11.63
5.25	6.18	6.33	6.48	6.64	6.82	7.00	7.19	7.50	7.84	8.20	8.61	9.05	9.55	10.29	11.39	12.21
5.50	6.47	6.63	6.79	6.96	7.14	7.33	7.53	7.86	8.21	8.59	9.02	9.48	10.00	10.78	11.94	12.79
5.75	6.76	6.93	7.10	7.28	7.47	7.67	7.88	8.21	8.58	8.98	9.43	9.91	10.45	11.27	12.48	13.37
6.00	7.06	7.23	7.41	7.59	7.79	8.00	8.22	8.57	8.96	9.38	9.84	10.34	10.91	11.76	13.02	13.95
6.50	7.65	7.83	8.02	8.22	8.44	8.67	8.90	9.29	9.70	10.16	10.64	11.21	11.82	12.75	14.11	15.12
7.00	8.24	8.43	8.64	8.86	9.09	9.33	9.59	10.00	10.45	10.94	11.46	12.07	12.73	13.73	15.19	16.28
7.50	8.82	9.04	9.26	9.49	9.74	10.00	10.27	10.71	11.19	11.72	12.28	12.93	13.64	14.71	16.28	17.44
8.00	9.41	9.64	9.88	10.12	10.39	10.67	10.96	11.43	11.94	12.50	13.10	13.79	14.55	15.69	17.36	18.60
8.50	10.00	10.24	10.49	10.76	11.04	11.33	11.64	12.14	12.69	13.28	13.92	14.66	15.45	16.67	18.45	19.77
9.00	10.59	10.84	11.11	11.39	11.69	12.00	12.33	12.86	13.43	14.06	14.74	15.52	16.36	17.65	19.53	20.93

DANGER!
Money Key No. 33

Watch out for
the hidden trap when you buy bonds

The disadvantage:

What you do when you buy bonds is settle for a fixed rate of return for a fixed period of time. When you buy a corporate bond paying 9% and maturing in 20 years, you should expect 9% per year (taxable) for the next 20 years. Likewise, with a municipal bond paying 7% per year and maturing in 24 years, you should look forward to a guaranteed 7% tax-free return each year for the next 24 years. But what should happen and what does happen are two different things. Bond dealers don't necessarily tell you about the hidden trap when you buy bonds.

This is it: Bond interest rates vary with the money markets. If interest rates in general drop while you hold a bond, you'll still earn at the fixed rate at which you bought the bond. That would be greater than the rate to which bonds had fallen —and you'd be ahead of the game. So *you* think.

If interest rates drop to any great extent, you probably wouldn't be allowed to hold your bond for the full term of 20 or 24 years or whatever the fixed period until maturity. Why should the bond issuer pay you 6, 7, 8, or 10% for many years to come if he can replace those high-interest bonds with a new issue paying 3 or 4%? What the bond issuer does is redeem your bond *before* maturity. (Bonds redeemable this way are

145

callable bonds; they can be *called* in.) The bond issuer takes the big payoff away from you.

How to get rid of this disadvantage:

There is a way to avoid the hidden trap: Don't buy any bond unless it's guaranteed against redemption—that is to say, guaranteed against being called in—for the full term to maturity. This is particularly important when you consider the purchase of bonds now being issued or bonds issued within the past few years. These bonds carry high interest rate coupons: taxable corporates at about 8 to 12%; tax-exempt municipals at about 4 to 9%. Some of these bonds have no call protection: they can be redeemed at any time. Some have limited call protection: they can't be redeemed for a fixed time—say five years from original issue date. Other bonds are *noncallable*. These are bonds that *cannot* be called in before maturity. They're the bonds you want.

When you stick to the noncallable bonds:

• You settle for a fixed yield for a fixed period of time.

• If bond prices drop and you sell, you lose. But you don't plan to sell. Remember, you've settled for a fixed interest rate for a fixed period of time.

• If bond prices rise and you sell, you make a capital gain. If you don't sell, you continue to earn the rate you've settled for—which is higher than interest rates offered on new bond issues. That's because when bond prices rise, interest rates decline.

TOP SECRET

Money Key No. 34

How to buy a 2.8% bond and come out with a yield of 6.88%—after taxes

The advantage:

There are billions of dollars' worth of bonds issued years ago carrying coupons paying 2.75, 3, or 3.5% per year. They are available through stockbrokers. Prices are quoted daily in the better newspapers. Municipal bonds not listed are available in huge quantities through brokers who specialize in such bonds and carry large portfolios in stock for quick delivery.

Why buy bonds paying around 2.75 to 3.5% when you can buy recently issued bonds paying 8 to 12% (taxable) or 4 to 9% (tax-exempt)?

How to use this advantage to make money:

Let's look at a good example. On May 5, 1970, a leading broker quoted a price of 78.265 (plus interest from January 1, 1970) for 2.8% California State Construction Bonds (tax-exempt) maturing July 1, 1976. The actual price you would have paid that day for those bonds was $782.65 (quoted as 78.265) plus $10.19 (interest from January 1, 1970, to May 5, 1970, at 2.8%). These bonds have a face value of $1,000 and carry clipable coupons of $14 payable every January 1 and July 1 through July 1, 1976. That $14 coupon, twice a year, adds up to $28, or 2.8% based on the $1,000 face value of the bond. However, the $1,000 bond cost only $782.65; on the basis of $782.65, $28 per year figures to be an interest rate of about 3.55%

The broker quoted the bond at "725.00 basis." That means that the yield to maturity, based on a price of $782.65, comes to 7.25%. Why this increased yield? That's because when the bond matures on July 1, 1976, you get the face value of the bond, $1,000—not the $782.65 you paid. You make a capital gain of $217.35 on your investment of $782.65, a gain of about 28% in just over 6 years *in addition to* the tax-free yield of 3.55%.

Now let's examine these figures to see what you really earn:

The quoted yield to maturity is	7.25%
The tax-free interest yield is	3.55%
Subtract and you get	3.70%

That 3.70% is the capital gain yield, taxable at about half rates. Therefore, only half the capital gain yield (at most) is fully taxable. Half of 3.70% is 1.85%. So

The tax-free interest yield is	3.55%
The nontaxable capital gain yield is	1.85%
Add and you get	5.40%

That 5.40% is the total tax-free yield. When you add

The total tax-free yield	5.40%
Taxable part of the capital gain yield	1.85%
You get the total yield to maturity	7.25%

To calculate your real yield, refer to your true ITB. If your true ITB is 50%, the tax on your capital gain reduces the yield by 50% of 1.85%, or 0.93%. 7.25% less 0.93% equals 6.32%, which is your true yield.

If your true ITB is, like most taxpayers', 20%, then the yield would be reduced by 20% of 1.85%, or 0.37%. 7.25% less 0.37% gives you your true yield of 6.88%.

If, at the time of maturity, you're retired and your true ITB is 0%, your yield is the full 7.25%.

So don't scorn old bond issues with low interest rates. They do pay off big. They pay off fast. And when you buy them, you not only virtually eliminate the danger of loss through premature redemption but you turn that danger to your advantage. That's because if yields go lower than your coupon rate (not too likely) and the bond *is* redeemed before maturity (usually with some premium), you earn your capital gain many years *before* maturity, increasing the yield greatly.

Money Key No. 35

Build your estate steadily—
with no chance of losing

The advantage:

Bond rates and bond prices vary from day to day, month to month, year to year. When bond rates drop, the price of bonds goes up. When bond rates go up, the price of bonds drops.

How to use this advantage to make money:

You can put your money in a bank and let it stay there at the advertised rates of interest, or you can work your money in and out of banks according to the MONEY KEYS. If you have an average true ITB of about 20%, your after-tax yield from working your money this way will often be greater than what you'd get from investments in tax-free bonds.

When bond rates drop below the yield offered by the use of the MONEY KEYS and the price of bonds goes up, sell your bonds and make a capital gain immediately. Put the money in your savings account and use the MONEY KEYS. Once more, you're getting yourself the highest return for your savings.

When bond rates go up again, bond prices fall. When bonds are yielding more than the yield you can obtain by using the MONEY KEYS, reinvest in bonds at the low prices to which they've fallen.

As bond yields rise and fall and as bond prices fall and

rise, by shifting back and forth between investments in bonds and the use of the MONEY KEYS in your banks you can *always* get the best possible return for your money—with safety. Your estate will grow steadily—with no chance of losing.

TOP SECRET
Money Key No. 36

How to reduce your income tax bracket without reducing your salary

The higher your true ITB, the greater a percentage of every dollar you earn is paid out in taxes. If your true ITB is 40%, it means that 40 cents out of every additional dollar that you make won't be yours. You'll take home only 60 cents. Obviously, it would be desirable to reduce your true ITB without reducing your salary. Can you do it? YES, YOU *CAN!*

The advantage:

If you have a sideline business, many of the goods and services you buy can be charged up as business expenses. The higher your ITB, the more valuable such charges are to you.

Whenever expenses are charged up as business expenses, you pay with *pre*tax dollars. When expenses are personal, you pay with *after*-tax dollars. To pay for $100 worth of business-deductible expenses, you need earn only $100. But to pay for $100 worth of nondeductible personal expenses, you need to earn *more* than $100. For example, if your true ITB is 50%, you have to earn $200 ($200 less 50% income tax equals $100 net available for payment of personal expenses).

How to use this advantage to make money:

It becomes obvious that a sideline business, any sideline business, that opens the door to taking deductible expenses can be highly profitable to the wage earner. How precisely?

Just bear this in mind: Every time you go to the theater, to a restaurant, to a resort, or travel on a plane, a lot of the people in those places are able to charge all their costs up to business expense—deductible from income for tax purposes, courtesy of the rules and regulations of our Internal Revenue Service.

A sideline business converts what would otherwise be non-deductible expenses into deductible expenses. The deductions come off your income, and your true ITB drops—as do your taxes. But your salary remains the same.

If your sideline business makes money, you're that much better off. If your sideline business loses money, you can still be better off—because what you save on personal taxes can be so much greater than what you lose on the business. Here's an example:

Let's suppose your business loss is $800, of which $700 was legitimate business expenses such as rent, telephone, postage, travel, bank charges, meals and entertainment. Let's also suppose, if you hadn't had the business, those expenses would have been personal expenses. Those personal expenses would not have been deductible, but with a sideline business, they are. If you're in the 30% income tax bracket, you can deduct $240 (30% × $800). Your true business expense is $800 less $700, or $100. You've lost $100 in your sideline business but gained $240 in tax savings for a net gain of $140.

You can make this place
a better place

At this point, I'd like to get away from the MONEY KEYS for a few sections.

Let's look into some of the social pressures we're subjected to and see how new ways of handling them—ways which may upset some of your prejudices—can improve your estate, your future, and possibly the lives of all of us.

We'll then return to the most important MONEY KEYS—*Keys* that will give you returns of 10.4, 16, 23.5%—and even an exceptional interest rate equivalent to 165%!

Charity can hurt you

Should you give to charity?

I'd like to tell you a story which could help you make up your mind.

I had a friend who worked for a fund-raising organization. A fund-raising organization is not an organized charity. It's a company that raises funds *for* an organized charity. My friend was a professional fund raiser. He gave me these facts:

A nationally known charitable organization (I won't mention names) contacted his fund-raising organization and said, "We want to raise money. How can you do it for us?"

The fund-raising organization suggested running a Madison Square Garden Evening of Stars. The funds would be raised by selling tickets.

To sell tickets to this kind of event isn't easy. What professional fund raisers do to make it easy is get a "name" with power behind it to back the show. A favorite "name" is that of a district director of Internal Revenue. Suppose somebody called you on the phone and said, "This is the office of Mr. So-and-So, the district director of Internal Revenue. We'd like you to take so-and-so-many tickets to the Evening of Stars," you'd think twice before saying no, wouldn't you? Using phone calls which sounded very much like that, the professional fund raisers had no trouble selling out the old Madison Square Garden, which seated about 22,000 people.

My friend invited me to that Evening of Stars, and I went. It was one of the big charity events of the year. A great many theatrical stars performed. The charity organization's committeewomen, with large orchids pinned on their dresses courtesy of the fund-raising organization, were beaming. And why shouldn't they? The show, I figured, must have brought in about *a quarter of a million dollars!*

I was bedazzled by the fact that a fund-raising organization could raise such an enormous sum for charity. Then my friend, who knew the story from the inside, went over the figures with me, and I began to see the situation clearly. My eyes were opened to a scandalous situation.

How much of that quarter of a million dollars do you think the charitable organization actually received? Let me show you where the money—money collected for charity—really went.

The individual fund raisers, the men and women like my friend who worked for the fund-raising organization, received 50% of the price of the tickets they sold. That's the way these fund raisers made their living.

The fund-raising organization's promoters received 25% of the funds raised. That was in return for all the work they did. After all, they organized the affair. They even provided orchids for the committeewomen, didn't they?

Madison Square Garden saw no reason why it should give its premises over to a charitable organization for nothing. The charitable organization had to pay full rental.

There were other production expenses as well. None of the suppliers offered discounts.

The stars who performed received no fees. But the rules of the charitable game required that amounts equal to the stars' fees had to be paid into retirement or benefits funds.

When all payments had been made, the charitable organization, which had sold over $250,000 worth of tickets, ended up with just under $3,000. *Of the $250,000 raised for charity, $247,000 went to people who certainly didn't need charity.*

The charitable organization *did* receive $3,000; but that didn't mean that all that $3,000 was used for charitable purposes. A good portion of that $3,000 went to the charitable organization's salaried personnel who make a living out of charities.

A quarter of a million dollars was raised *for* charity, but only a handful of dollars went *to* charity.

You listen to a national telethon, and you're ready to send off some of your hard-earned dollars. But before you do, consider:

A charitable organization is not likely to get more than pennies out of each dollar you donate. When you donate to an organized charity, what you're really doing is supporting people who make organized charity their business. Organized charity is probably the second largest industry in the nation.

Should you give to *organized* charity?

Your first charity should be your family. Provide for your family's future, your family's security. When you give to organized charity before that's done, you're hurting your family, because what you give you take from your estate.

If, after you've put aside enough for your family and you have some money left that you wish to donate to charity, why not use that money for something you really feel strongly about? How about helping a neighbor? Or helping the family of a fireman or policeman killed in the line of duty? Or helping send some bright child through school, so he can not only better himself but also make contributions to society and better the lives of all of us?

Giving this personal way—through your own *unorganized* charity—will give you the kind of pleasure you never get by handing your money over to some impersonal organized charity. Isn't that better than subsidizing an organized charity, which, too often, merely enables its promoters to enrich themselves?

Increase your buying power

Ten men produce 100 pieces of merchandise. The labor cost comes to $20 for each piece. Total labor cost is $2,000 (100 times $20).

Suppose these same 10 men produce not 100 pieces but 120 pieces. The labor cost per piece of merchandise comes down to $16.67, a cost decrease of 16.67%.

The increase in productivity cuts cost, and that cut can be passed on to the consumer. As production costs decrease, prices can decrease; the dollar can buy more.

Shouldn't the worker say to himself, "Instead of boondoggling on the job, shouldn't I work harder because that will bring the prices down and *I'll* live better?"

Beware: your raise is your loss

Most people want more. Most people have the attitude of "What's in it for me? Gimme! Gimme! Gimme! I want! I'll take! I must have!" But these people fool themselves. The more they get, the less they get. Let me tell you why:

These people have ensured the jobs of labor leaders who boast, "Look, I got you a 10% increase. Look how wonderful I am!" That sounds fine to these people. But what they don't realize is:

As costs go up, business increases prices to cover these costs. When wages go up, prices go up—and up and up and up—10, 20, 50% and higher. As a general rule, when wages double, prices double.

Does that mean the worker is no worse off than he was before? I think you're in for a surprise.

Let's take the case of a worker with a gross income of $10,000 per year. After taxes, assuming he lives in a state where there is a state tax levy, he ends up with take-home pay of $8,080. (I'm using New York State tax tables for my calculations. The general results are the same no matter what state tax tables are used.) The worker is able to buy $8,080 worth of goods and services—and let's say he buys them.

Let's assume his wages double. He's getting $20,000 per

year gross income. Prices also double. In order to buy the same amount of goods and services that he had been buying, he now has to have a *net* income double his previous net income, which would be $8,080 times 2, or $16,160. But while his *gross* income has doubled, his *net* income has *not*. The reason is:

As he makes more money, the government takes a greater percentage of that money. That's *progressive* taxation. As a result of progressive taxation, what's his net? About $14,400. That's about $2,000 *short* of the $16,160 he needs to buy as much as he did *before* his gross income doubled. Gimme! Gimme! Gimme! He *got*. And he lost about $2,000 in actual buying power.

The worker doesn't really profit from wage increases. Does anybody? Let's look at the corporation:

When wages double, corporation costs—for real estate, advertising, raw materials, and premanufactured products, for example—also double. What the corporation does as its costs double and its overhead doubles is to double its prices. The total profit of the corporation doubles. A corporation that made $1 million in profit doubles its profit to $2 million. But corporate taxation is not and has not been progressive. As a rule of thumb, corporation taxes run about 50% of profits—*always* about 50% of profits. No matter how much profit the company makes, that tax percentage does *not* increase. So as corporate gross profits double, so do corporate net (after tax) profits.

Contrast the corporation with the worker. When his salary doubles, his take-home pay does not double. In the example I've just given you, his take-home pay (after taxes) went up only 78%. But the corporation's profits went up 100%. When the workers, through their labor leaders, holler "Gimme! Gimme! Gimme! I want more from the corporation," and they get it, it's the workers who lose, not the corporation.

Let's take a situation in which salaries go down rather than up. The worker starts with a $20,000 per year income, and he's cut back to $10,000 per year. This happens during a general period of deflation.

Remember, with his $20,000 a year income, he was able to purchase $14,400 worth of goods and services. In a general period of deflation, as wages are cut in half, prices should be cut in half. He can now buy the same things that he bought for $14,400 for $7,200.

But what's his take-home pay? Thanks to the progressive income tax, the government takes a *smaller* percentage because he is earning less. His take-home pay is *more* than half of $14,400. It is, as I've already figured out for you, $8,080. *Although his salary was cut, he actually gained close to $900 in buying power* ($8,080 minus $7,200 = $880).

During the same period of deflation, the corporation, with its expenses cut in half and its prices cut in half, has its total profits cut in half. Since the corporate tax remains the same no matter what the profits, the net profits (after taxes) are also cut in half.

So if wages go down, prices should go down, and it's the worker who'll gain, not the corporation.

You see how the Gimme! Gimme! Gimme! attitude is hurting all of us? The worker has been fooled by numbers. It satisfies his ego to say, "I'm earning *twice* as much money now!" But he's actually earning *less* in buying power.

If the worker dropped his Gimme! Gimme! Gimme! attitude and utilized the power of his labor unions to *decrease* wages, increase productivity, and *force a decrease in prices proportionately,* so that when wages go down 10%, prices go down 10%, all of us could actually enjoy a *true* increase in buying power.

But these are changes for the future. In the meantime, to fight the constantly rising cost of living, you've got to get the most from your savings dollar. So let's get back to the MONEY KEYS.

DANGER!
Money Key No. 37

Watch out for
free checking accounts—
they cost a good deal of money

In recent years there's been a great deal of advertising about free checking accounts. Actually, they're free only if you maintain certain balances in the bank.

To maintain a free checking account, you need a minimum daily balance—*not* an average balance. That minimum daily balance is likely to be $500. That means your balance always has to be *more than* $500; because if just one check clears and drops your balance to $499.99, you're charged, and often charged heavily. In order for a $500 minimum balance to be really free, the odds are that over the year you'd have to maintain an average balance of $600.

You can readily see that $600 at 5% could be earning you $31 a year at 5% compounded continuously. If you were to earn more than 5%—and you know you can earn 6% easily with savings certificates or 10% or more by using the MONEY KEYS—you can see that the free checking account is not so free.

Money Key No. 38

How to cut the cost of your checking account

The advantage:

You know from the previous MONEY KEY that free checking accounts cost you money. You also know from your own experience that special checking accounts cost you money.

Here's your advantage: special checking accounts may cost you *less* money than free checking accounts.

How to use this advantage to save money:

First, determine *your* cost per check for a special checking account. It's simple to do.

Start by going to your checkbook and counting up the number of checks that you used during the past year—from January 1 through December 31. Now, add up the total cost of your special checking account for that year: the cost per check plus monthly charges. Divide the total cost by the number of checks you've drawn, and that will give you your cost per check for special checking.

Now, determine the cost per check for a free checking account:

Figure how much interest you would have lost if you had maintained your minimum balance plus the safety margin (See previous MONEY KEY). Calculate the lost interest on the basis of the interest-bearing account of your choice or on the basis of your use of the MONEY KEYS. However calculated, the loss of interest is the real cost of your free checking. Divide that cost by the number of checks you've drawn last year, and that will give you the cost per check for free checking.

Compare your cost per check for special checking with your cost per check for free checking. Select the kind of checking which gives you the lower cost per check.

As a rule of thumb, if you don't use a lot of checks, the special checking account ends up cheaper than the free checking account.

However, if you find a bank that offers you a really free checking account, that is, a checking account that requires *no* minimum balance—or if you find a bank that requires only a small minimum balance like $100—then the free checking account is likely to be cheaper than the special account.

Whichever type of account you use, you pay the total costs out of your after-tax earnings. But if you have a sideline business (See MONEY KEY No. 36) and use your business checking account to pay your bills, the cost of maintaining that checking account is a business cost and is, therefore, tax deductible.

I'll tell you more about checking account advantages in later MONEY KEYS.

Money Key No. 39

Get your money faster

The advantages:

In some banks, when you take your paycheck to the teller's window, deposit the whole check, and then want to withdraw a portion of that deposit, you may be hit by a bank rule stating that checks cannot be drawn against for four business days, ten business days, or even for an entire month. The business days that must elapse before a check can be drawn against are known as "clearance days." During these clearance days when your money is tied up, it's the same as if you didn't have that money. When you need funds, the number of days your funds are tied up is important to you.

Here are several facts that may help you get the use of your income faster:

• Clearance days vary from bank to bank. Generally a business bank will give clearance faster than a savings bank or savings and loan association.

• Most state laws require that when an employee is paid by check, he should be able to convert it to cash immediately. Therefore, employers usually arrange with a bank convenient to the employee to cash payroll checks with no time required for clearance. Often, a bank will provide employees of large companies with identification cards so that their payroll checks can be cashed in the bank upon presentation of the cards.

• Once you are known to your local bank, the bank is likely to cash checks made payable to you by financially sound institutions without any clearance time.

Little thing? Not when the unforeseen emergency arises and you need money fast.

How to use these advantages to get money faster:

• Shop for minimum clearance days. Simply go to the banks in your neighborhood and ask bank officers, "How long will it take my paycheck to clear?" Favor the bank that offers the least number of clearance days.

• Make arrangements with the bank of your choice to the effect that, if the checks you deposit are drawn on well-established companies, government agencies, or other sound financial institutions, these checks will be accepted as cash and you will be allowed to draw against them immediately.

• Get yourself an identification card that will permit you to cash your payroll check at a particular bank.

Money Key No. 40

Pay to the order of . . .
with free checks and money orders

The advantage:

How do you pay your bills? I have seen many people go up to a bank teller and buy money orders which cost 10 to 25 cents. Other people draw checks against their special or regular checking account. The cost of maintaining such accounts can amount to sizable sums of money by the end of the year.

Instead of paying for money orders or checks, why not take advantage of a benefit offered with many savings accounts? These accounts permit you to draw a number of checks or money orders in place of cash. In some accounts, the number of checks or money orders you can draw is unlimited—no charge for this service.

How to use this advantage to save money:

When you're ready to pay a bill, say to the telephone company, make out a withdrawal slip on your savings account for the amount you need, but don't take cash. Ask for a check or money order. It's free with many savings accounts.

In most banks, the teller will make out the check to whomever you please. You can have him make it out to the telephone company. But you're safer having the check made out to yourself, writing on the back, "Pay to the order of ABC Telephone

Co.," and signing your name. If the check is lost, the bank can stop payment on it.

If you have a special checking account as well as a savings account, remember that every check you draw costs you money. Use the *free* checks or money orders instead.

TOP SECRET

Money Key No. 41

How to make money when you pay your bills

The advantage:

There are certain bills you have to pay month in and month out. These include rent, mortgage, insurance, electricity, and telephone. Many people take enough out of each paycheck to take care of some of these bills as well as their credit card bills. These people pay as their income comes in.

However, it is highly advantageous to take care of all your bills at one time during the month—say at the end of the month. Let's see what this can do for you as far as building your estate is concerned.

How to use this advantage to make money:

Let's assume you have $800 worth of bills you could pay at the end of each month.

First of all, set aside $200 a week to cover this $800. In a day of deposit to day of withdrawal account, you earn interest on your money for every day it's in the bank. Now let's see how much you can earn in interest in the course of a year when you deposit that $200 weekly. (Of course, your weekly deposits could be $20, $2,000, or any sum; the principle is the same.)

Let's start arbitrarily with the beginning of the calendar year 1973 and assume that you get your paycheck on Fridays.

On Friday, January 5, deposit $200 into your day of deposit to day of withdrawal account.

On Friday, January 12, deposit another $200. That brings your balance to $400.

On Friday, January 19, deposit another $200, which brings your balance to $600.

Friday, January 26, is very close to the end of the month, and if you deposited your paycheck on that date, the check might not clear by January 31. So don't deposit your paycheck but take $200 in cash, withdraw $600 from your savings account, and deposit a total of $800 in your checking account. (Or convert the money into free checks or money orders if you prefer to pay your bills that way.)

What did you accomplish?

You had $200 in the bank for 21 days, another $200 in the bank for 14 days, and another $200 in the bank for 7 days. During that month, your average balance came to about $280. On an average balance of $280, at 5% day of deposit to day of withdrawal compounded continuously (which gives a yield of 5.2%), you earn about $14.50 on an annual basis.

It's not a great deal of money, but it's found money. It's money you wouldn't have had if you'd paid your bills out of your paycheck each week.

TOP SECRET

Money Key No. 42

How to almost double the money you make when you pay your bills

The advantage:

In the MONEY KEY I've just gone over with you, I showed you how to make money when you pay your bills. On monthly bills of $800, the money you make amounts to about $14.50 on an annual basis.

Let's establish a program for a full quarter to get the most out of your savings.

How to use this advantage to make money:

Once again, lets start from the beginning of the year. On Fridays, January 5, 12, and 19, deposit $200 into your day of deposit to day of withdrawal account. On January 26, *deposit* $200. Wait until January 31 to withdraw the $800 you need to pay your bills.

Caution: On that last deposit, until the bank gets to know you and gets to know that your paycheck is good, it may be desirable to cash your paycheck in the issuing bank and deposit $200 in cash in your savings account to be sure those funds will be available to you on January 31.

On January 31, withdraw the $800. (Remember to maintain the minimum balance required by your bank. When I refer to your balance in this MONEY KEY, for the sake of simplicity, I'm disregarding that minimum balance or whatever other funds you have in your account.)

On Friday, February 2, which is only two days after you made your withdrawal of $800, deposit $200, bringing your balance to $200. On February 9, 16, and 23, do the same thing. Your balance is now up to $800. At the end of February, on the twenty-eighth, withdraw your $800, put it into your checking account, write your checks, and send them off. Your balance is zero.

On March 2, deposit $200. Make $200 deposits on March 9, 16, 23, *and* 30. By March 30 you have a balance of *$1,000* in your account. On March 31, withdraw the $800 you need for your checking account. *Now, at the end of the quarter, without the interest you've earned, you have an extra $200 ($1,000 minus $800).*

That $200 is found money. If you had that $200 in cash in your pocket, the odds are that you would have spent it on impulse buying. Of course, that $200 is available to you should you want to or need to use it. But the fact that the money is in the bank tends to keep you from spending it frivolously. As a fringe benefit of this program, you've saved $200 in one quarter.

Let's see what you earned during that quarter. Remember there are two types of day of deposit to day of withdrawal accounts. One type pays you only from day of deposit to day of withdrawal. The other type, offered by a numerous banks or savings and loan associations, like the West Side Federal Savings and Loan Association in New York City and the Prudential Federal Savings & Loan Association in Salt Lake City, not only pays you from day of deposit to day of withdrawal but also gives you the grace and bonus days that other banks only offer on their regular savings accounts. Depending on which of these two types of accounts you have, you earn between $23 and $24 on an annual basis during the quarter.

In the previous MONEY KEY, I showed you that the use of the day of deposit to day if withdrawal account at 5% compounded continuously gives an annual yield of about $14.50. Therefore, your earnings of $23 to $24 are equivalent to a yield of approximately 8%—a sizable increase over 5%, as $23 to $24 is a sizable increase over $14.50.

In the next MONEY KEY, I'll show you how to double that yield.

TOP SECRET

Money Key No. 43

How to earn 16%

The advantage:

You must make use of a very special type of account that is available, to the best of my knowledge, in only one bank in the country. However, this account has become so popular over the past 10 years that this bank reports it has more than 190,000 account holders in the 50 states of the Union and in 37 foreign nations. If a bank can attract accounts from so many people from so many areas, it must have something special to offer. Let's examine what this bank offers.

The account is called the United Security Account—or USA account. It's offered only by the Citizens Bank and Trust Company of Park Ridge, Chicago, Illinois. The title United Security Account is registered with the United States Patent Office and may not be used without license by any other bank, trust company, or savings institution. Citizens Bank describes its United Security Account as the only bank account plan in America that pays the highest interest and permits the depositor to write checks free.

What Citizens Bank has done is combine a checking account with a savings account. In the checking account, you keep no balance at all. Your savings account is collateral for any checks that you write.

Example: You have a balance of $800 in your savings account. You write a check for $200. The bank pays the check and marks up on its records that you owe $200. If you pay back that $200 by the fifteenth of the month following the month in which your check clears, Citizens Bank will have loaned you that $200 with no interest or service charges whatsoever. If you don't repay that loan by the fifteenth, then, of course, you'll have to pay interest.

The checks you write are never deducted from your savings balance, which pays 4.5%. *You continue to earn interest on your full balance even though you're drawing against it.*

The checks cost you nothing if you use 15 or less a month. If you use more than 15 a month, the additional ones cost you 15 cents apiece. A zero-balance checking account with 15 free checks each month is among the cheapest checking accounts you could possibly have. The checks are just as good as any other checks anywhere in the United States, or in the world for that matter. The savings accounts are fully insured to $20,000 by the FDIC. Citizens Bank provides you with a regular monthly statement which shows you the amount of your savings and the amount that you owe to the bank for checks you have written. The bank calls its check loans "advancing of check credit."

The USA account is a brilliantly simple concept which should be extremely attractive to any savings-conscious individual.

To open a USA account, you can either fill out the coupon in the bank's ad, which appears from time to time in nationally distributed media, or you can request an application directly from the bank. According to the bank, applications are accepted only when there is space available on its computers. It's possible that you may have to wait to get your account. But as the USA account has increased in popularity, the bank has periodically opened large blocks of accounts, so the odds are now good that accounts are available or will be available in short order.

How to use this advantage to make money:
    Open a USA account.
    Asssume the same conditions as in the previous two MONEY KEYS. But instead of depositing your $200 each week in a local day of deposit to day of withdrawal account, make your deposits in your USA account.
    STEP No. 1. Deposit the first $200 on January 5. On January 12, deposit another $200. This brings your balance, except for the minimum balance with which you opened your account, to $400. On January 19, deposit another $200, and on January 26, $200 more. That brings your balance to $800.
    (At this point, I want to give you a word of caution. You may be maintaining your USA account from some distant point relative to the bank. Under those circumstances, ordinary checks would take time to clear. There would be a delay before such checks, deposited by you, could be used as collateral against your USA checks. To avoid this, make your deposits in the form of teller's checks, certified checks, or money orders. If you're paid with a government check, you can make your deposit with it, since such checks are regarded as cash in a USA account.)
    On January 31, using the free imprinted checkbook supplied you by the bank, write out checks totaling $800 to cover your monthly expenses, just as you did when you were using the two previous MONEY KEYS. In any other account, your balance would be zero except for your initial deposit. But not in this account. Your savings balance *still* shows $800.
    Shortly after the end of the month you receive a statement of your USA account as of January 31. The checks you wrote

and sent out on January 31 have not cleared, so your first statement shows a savings balance of $800 and a check credit bal-
ance used of zero. Those checks amounting to $800 should clear
during the month of February. When they do, your account *at*
the bank (you haven't received the second statement yet) will
show that you have $800 of savings and $800 of check credit
in use.

Remember, as long as you repay that $800 by the fifteenth
of the month following the month in which the checks for that
amount clear—in other words, as long as the $800 is repaid by
March 15—there are no charges whatsoever for this checking
service.

STEP NO. 2. You have a day of deposit to day of withdrawal account in a local savings bank or savings and loan
institution.

Deposit $200 in that account on Friday, February 2. Your
balance is then $200 above what you already had in the ac-
count. Make deposits of $200 on the next two Fridays, Feb-
ruary 9 and 16. On February 23, deposit another $200, bringing
your balance to $800.

On February 27—that's long before March 15—withdraw
$800 by means of a teller's check or a bank check from your
day of deposit to day of withdrawal account. Send that $800 to
your USA account to repay your $800 worth of check loans.
The payment will arrive at Citizens Bank on February 28 or
March 1 and is credited as cash immediately.

So between February 28 and March 1 the bank records
would show that you have $800 in savings and you *had* $800 in
check credit which you repaid, bringing your check credit in
use back to zero. You again have $800 available for writing
checks.

STEP NO. 3. On February 28, write out your monthly
checks and mail them off. Sometime during March, they'll
clear through your USA account. The bank records will show,

as they did the month before, $800 worth of savings and $800 worth of check credit in use.

Now back to your local day of deposit to day of withdrawal account: On March 2 and again on March 9, 16, and 23, deposit $200, bringing your balance to $800. On March 29, withdraw $800 by teller's check and send it to Citizens Bank to repay the check loans on your USA account.

On Friday, March 30, deposit the last $200 for March in your day of deposit to day of withdrawal account. At the end of March you have $200 left in that account. As in MONEY KEY No. 42, the extra $200 you saved is found money. Using your savings account according to this program, you put money that would ordinarily have gone into your pocket and out again into a bank instead. You've also earned interest on both your day of deposit to day of withdrawal and your USA account.

Let's see what you earned this quarter, on an annual basis.

First, your USA account. During your first month, you started with nothing. (Remember, for the sake of simplicity we're not considering your basic balance in any of these calculations.) You deposited $200, then a week later another $200, and so on. During your first month, you had an average balance of $368. Your second and third months showed an average balance to $800. Your average balance over the quarter works out to about $656. The interest you earned for this quarter on that $656 comes to $7.50, give or take a few cents. On an annual basis that's about $30.

Now your day of deposit to day of withdrawal account. During this quarter, you added nothing to this account in the first month. In the next two months, February and March, you earned just about $4 on your money. That's about $16 on an annual basis.

Adding the $30 you earned on the USA account to the $16

you earned on the day of deposit to day of withdrawal account gives you total earnings of about $46 on an annual basis.

Recall that on a program of $200-a-week deposits in a day of deposit to day of withdrawal account (see MONEY KEY No. 41), the yield on an annual basis was about $14.50 at 5%. Since you earned about $46 instead of about $14.50, your yield is more than three times that of 5%—equivalent to a yield of about 16%.

In the next MONEY KEY, I'll show you how to get an even higher yield.

TOP SECRET

Money Key No. 44

How to earn 23.5%

The advantage:
Continue the program of the preceding MONEY KEY for another quarter.

How to use this advantage to make money:
During April, May, and June, always maintain a savings balance of $800 in your USA account in Citizens Bank. At 4.5% interest compounded semiannually, $800 yields interest of about $37 on an annual basis.

In your day of deposit to day of withdrawal account, the average balance over the second quarter—provided your account gives the grace and bonus days that West Side Federal does—will come to something like $606. The interest on $606 is about $31 on an annual basis. (If your day of deposit to day of withdrawal account does not offer these monthly grace and bonus days, the yield will be slightly smaller, but not sufficiently smaller to concern you.)

Add your earnings on both accounts (about $37 plus about $31) and you get a total of about $68.

Remember that $14.50 is the yield for 5% (see MONEY KEY

No. 41). Earnings of $68 on an annual basis are equivalent to a yield of 23.5%.

You may think $68 is not a great deal of money. But that's $68 you would not have earned at all had you continued paying your bills as your paychecks came in. And it is $54 *more* than you would have earned had you just put your paycheck into a day of deposit to day of withdrawal account and paid your bills at the end of the month. It's $68 that's added to your estate at the end of the year.

TOP SECRET

Money Key No. 45

An exceptional interest rate of 165%

The advantages:

It's really quite simple to arrange for a cash reserve. If you have a checking account and your bank offers cash reserve, just ask for a cash reserve application, fill it out, and if you're credit-worthy, your bank will assign a cash reserve to you of between $500 and $5,000. I anticipate that the $5,000 ceiling will be raised very shortly to $10,000. Actually, your cash reserve can be greater than $5,000 even now. There's no reason why you can't have a cash reserve in two checking accounts, or in three or more.

Let me refresh your memory about cash reserve.

Cash reserve (it goes by different names in many banks) permits you to write checks up to the amount of your cash reserve even though you have insufficient funds in your account to cover the checks. For example, you want to buy an appliance for $429. You have only $29 in the bank. You write a check for $429, and the bank automatically advances you the difference between the $29 you have and the $429 you need. You now owe the bank $400 ($429 minus $29) and you pay for it at a rate of 12% per year. You can continue to write checks up to

185

your cash reserve ceiling. In many banks, the moment you make a deposit in your checking account, you automatically repay part of the cash advanced. If you don't use your cash reserve, it costs you nothing. (Caution: In some banks you must repay cash advances separately from deposits to avoid excessive interest charges.)

Remember that cash reserve offers the same kind of temptation that the credit card does—the temptation to buy now and worry about paying later. As a reader of this book, you know that the credit card is a useful but dangerous tool. Use it, but be careful of it; don't let it explode in your face. So with cash reserve. It's a highly valuable tool. Make use of it. But don't let it abuse you.

I've already told you about one way you can use your cash reserve in connection with your credit card to save money (see MONEY KEY No. 26). Now I'd like to show you how to combine the advantages of cash reserve, credit cards, a day of deposit to day of withdrawal account, and a USA account to get an astonishing rate of interest.

How to use these advantages to make money:

Let's assume the billing date on your credit card is the fifth; your payment date is the thirtieth. Let's also assume that on January 5, you charge a $500 TV set with your credit card. The charge will not appear on your bill until the fifth of the following month—February 5. You don't have to pay until March 2.

On March 1, write out a check for $500 on your USA account and mail the check so that it arrives on March 2 at the credit card company.

The check doesn't clear out of your USA account until later in March. Your listed check credit in use in that account is now $500. You must repay that $500 by April 15.

Before April 15, say on April 13, write a local check against your cash reserve to repay your check loan of $500 in your USA account. Some time between April 17 and April 21, make a deposit in your checking account to cover the cash reserve advance. Do this by means of a withdrawal from your local day of deposit to day of withdrawal account.

What's it all add up to?

Although you made your purchase on January 5, you didn't touch any of your savings to pay for it until around April 17–21. *You received over a hundred days of free credit.*

Or look at it this way: You could have purchased the $500 TV set on February 5 and paid for it on delivery on Thursday, February 8, with cash. Between the fifth and the eighth, the money you had already spent could have continued to earn money for you in your day of deposit to day of withdrawal account. You could have earned three days of interest. But by using your credit card, your USA account, your cash reserve, and your local day of deposit to day of withdrawal savings account, you earned a little over 100 days of interest on the same transaction. That's 33 times as much interest. If you earned 5% interest in your day of deposit to day of withdrawal account, then 33 times that is 165%.

None of this could have been accomplished if you didn't have $500 in your USA account as well as $500 in your local savings account. You can see the advantage of not keeping all your money locally at 5%. It's more profitable for you to keep part of your money at Citizens Bank and Trust in Chicago at 4.5%.

TOP SECRET

Money Key No. 46

Earn 10.4% on your savings
every day of the year

The advantage:

An interesting situation arose toward the end of 1971 in New York City. Financial experts of the city government conducted a test to determine the minimum average number of days it takes for checks issued by the city to clear. When they found this minimum average clearance time, they put it to use in an utterly new way. *The city government issued checks against insufficient funds in its checking accounts.*

There *were* sufficient New York City funds in interest-bearing instruments. But these funds were not drawn out and transferred to the checking accounts to cover the checks issued until the end of the average clearance time. *For the number of days it took the checks to clear, the city of New York was earning interest on the total amount drawn on those checks.* According to a report in *The New York Times,* New York City earned $15.5 million dollars in this way during one year.

Can you do what New York City did by writing checks first and depositing the money to cover them later? YES, YOU CAN. On a smaller scale, of course—using cash reserve.

Start by determining the average minimum clearance date

of your checks. Here's a simple way to do it:

During any two weeks in a month, write a check every day, Monday through Friday, and deposit it into your savings account. Key each check by writing in a number of pennies to correspond with the date. For example, on the check issued on January 13, write in the amount $10.*13;* on the check for January 14, write in $12.14; and so on. When you get your statement at the end of the month, it will be easy to see how many days it took any check to clear. Example:

Want to find out how long it took the check you deposited on January 13 to clear? Just look at your statement and see what day a check with an amount ending in 13 cents cleared. If you find it cleared on January 16, you know it took three days to clear.

You'll probably find that you'll have no difficulty obtaining a minimum average time of three to four business days, particularly if your savings account is in a savings and loan association.

How to use this advantage to make money:

Let's assume that you've found that the average minimum time it takes for a check you've written and deposited in your savings account to clear is three days.

STEP No. 1. Let's assume the balance in your checking account is $100 (A in Step 1 Chart), and you have a balance of $2,001 in your savings (B in the Step 1 Chart). (The figures are arbitrary; you could use any sums.)

Let's further assume that this program is taking place in February, 1973. (The program works just as well in any month, but I've selected this month as an example because it includes three-day weekends as well as two-day weekends.)

On February 1, write a check for $2,000.01 on your checking account even though you have a balance of only $100 in that account (C in the Step 1 Chart). By writing a check for

Step 1 Chart

DAY OF DEPOSIT TO DAY OF WITHDRAWAL
SAVINGS ACCOUNT

Date	CHECKING ACCOUNT (Balance = $100) (A)						
	Check Clears Deposit to cover checks	Checks written	Deposit	Withdraw	Balance	Deposit clears (6 bus. days)	Date check can be made (3 bus. days)
Wed. 1/31/73					(B) 2000.01		
Thurs. 2/1/73		(C) 2000.01	(D) 2000.01		(E) 4001.01		
Fri. 2					4001.01		
Sat. 3					4001.01		
Sun. 4					4001.01		
Mon. 5							
Tues. 6	(G) 2000.01			(H) 2000.01	2001.00		2/6
Wed. 7					No! See (L) in step		
Thurs. 8					2 chart		
Fri. 9							
Sat. 10						(F)	

$2,000.01 rather than a round figure of $2,000, you can easily follow exactly what happens as the check is processed. Key other checks in the same way, with the cents figure corresponding to the date of issue.

On the same day, February 1, put the check for $2,000.01 in your saving account (D in Step 1 Chart). That brings the balance of your savings account, which was $2,001, to $4,000.01 (E in Step 1 Chart). You immediately start earning interest on that new balance. The $2,001.01 that you deposited is not available for withdrawal, according to your saving account regulations, until six business days later, on February 9 (F in Step 1 Chart).

Now let's go back to the check you drew for $2,000.01 on February 1 (C on Step 1 Chart). Since you have determined that it will take three business days for that check to clear out of your checking account, you must be able to make a deposit of $2,000.01 into your checking account three business days after the first, which is February 6 (G in Step 1 Chart). How do you do this? In your savings account, the original balance of $2,001 (B in Step 1 Chart) has been available to you all the time. So on February 6, withdraw $2,000.01 from your savings account (H in Step 1 Chart) and deposit it in your checking account on the sixth (G in Step 1 Chart).

What you've been doing over this short period is drawing interest on $4,001.01 even though you have only $2,001! Let's see if you can continue to do this.

Step No. 2. You know that the deposit you made into your savings account on February 1 (D in Step 1 Chart) will be available to you on February 9 (F in Step 1 Chart).

That means you can make a deposit into your checking account on February 9. You can, therefore, write a check three business days before you make that deposit on February 9. Three business days before February 9 is February 6. Write that check, keying it at $2,000.06 (I in Step 2 Chart) and de-

Step 2 Chart

	CHECKING ACCOUNT (Balance = $100)		DAY OF DEPOSIT TO DAY OF WITHDRAWAL SAVINGS ACCOUNT				
Date	Check Clears Deposit to cover checks	Checks written	Deposit	Withdraw	Balance	Deposit clears (6 bus. days)	Date check can be made (3 bus. days)
Mon. 5							
Tues. 6		(I) 2000.06	(J) 2000.06	2000.01 (L)	(K) 4001.01 / (L) 4001.06		
Wed. 7					4001.06		
Thurs. 8					4001.06		
Fri. 9	(O) 2000.06			(N) 2000.06	2001.00 — No! See in step 3 chart (R)		2/9
Sat. 10							
Sun. 11							
Mon. 12							
Tues. 13						(M)	
Wed. 14							
Thurs. 15							
Fri. 16							
Sat. 17							

posit it in your savings account (J in Step 2 Chart).

You just withdrew $2,000.01 from your savings account (H in Step 1 Chart), but *on the same day* deposit $2,000.06 (J in Step 2 Chart). So your savings account, which had remained at $4,001.01 from February 1 through February 5 (K in Step 2 Chart), now becomes $4,001.06 (L in Step 2 Chart).

On February 9, withdraw $2,000.06 from your savings account (N in Step 2 Chart) and on the same day deposit it into your checking account (O in Step 2 Chart). That deposit covers the check drawn on February 6 (I in Step 2 Chart).

The deposit of $2,000.06 you made in your savings account on February 6 (J in Step 2 Chart) will be available to you for withdrawal six business days later, or on February 15 (M in Step 2 Chart). However, three business days prior to that, you can write a check against the soon-to-be-available funds.

Step No. 3. On February 9, write a check for $2,000.09 (P in Step 3 Chart) and deposit that in your savings account (Q in Step 3 Chart).

So, on February 9, you've withdrawn $2,000.06 from your savings account (N in Step 2 Chart) and deposited $2,000.09 in your savings account (Q in Step 3 Chart). Your balance in your savings account remains virtually the same except that it increases by 3 cents to $4,001.09 (R in Step 3 Chart).

Step 3 Chart

Date		CHECKING ACCOUNT (Balance = $100)		DAY OF DEPOSIT TO DAY OF WITHDRAWAL SAVINGS ACCOUNT			
		Check Clears Deposit to cover checks	Checks written	Deposit	Withdraw	Balance	Deposit clears (6 bus. days)	Date check can be made (3 bus. days)
Fri.	9		(P) 2000.09	(Q) 2000.09	2000.06 (R) 4001.09		
Sat.	10						
Sun.	11						
Mon.	12						
Tues.	13						
Wed.	14						
Thurs.	15	2000.09			2000.09		2/15
Fri.	16						
Sat.	17						
Sun.	18						
Mon.	19						
Tues.	20						

You can repeat this program indefinitely.

What this program demonstrates is that, day after day after day, your savings account can maintain a balance of double your original, or "real," balance. That means you're earning on double the amount of money. If your savings account is paying you 5% compounded continuously with a yield of 5.2%, you'll be getting a return every day of the year of 10.4%. *Your estate grows twice as fast!*

If you have a "free" checking account, all those checks are yours to use without additional cost.

In case you have any reservations about issuing checks against insufficient funds, you can use the cash reserve feature of your checking account. That puts the bank's official stamp of approval on those checks you issue without having enough money to cover them. Laws concerning issuance of checks against insufficient funds vary from state to state. But no legal problem concerning the issuance of such checks arises in any state provided you do not issue checks in excess of the sum of your cash balance plus your cash reserve.

HOW TO EARN 10.4% ON YOUR SAVINGS EVERY DAY OF THE YEAR

(Step 1 Chart, Step 2 Chart, and Step 3 Chart Combined.)

	CHECKING ACCOUNT (Balance = $100)			DAY OF DEPOSIT TO DAY OF WITHDRAWAL SAVINGS ACCOUNT				
Date	Check Clears Deposit to cover checks	Checks written		Deposit	Withdraw	Balance	Deposit clears (6 bus. days)	Date check can be made (3 bus. days)
Wed. 1/31/73						2000.01		
Thurs. 2/1/73		2000.01		2000.01		4001.01		
Fri. 2						4001.01		
Sat. 3						4001.01		
Sun. 4						4001.01		
Mon. 5						4001.01		
Tues. 6	2000.01	2000.06		2000.06	2000.01	4001.06		2/6
Wed. 7						4001.06		
Thurs. 8						4001.06		
Fri. 9	2000.06	2000.09		2000.09	2000.06	4001.09		2/9
Sat. 10						4001.09		

Day						
Sun. 11					4001.09	
Mon. 12					4001.09	
Tues. 13					4001.09	
Wed. 14					4001.09	
Thurs. 15	2000.09	2000.15	2000.15	2000.09	4001.15	2/15
Fri. 16					4001.15	
Sat. 17					4001.15	
Sun. 18					4001.15	
Mon. 19					4001.15	
Tues. 20					4001.15	
Wed. 21	2000.15	2000.21	2000.21	2000.15	4001.21	2/21
Thurs. 22					4001.21	
Fri. 23					4001.21	
Sat. 24					4001.21	
Sun. 25					4001.21	
Mon. 26	2000.21	2003.26	2000.26	2000.21	4001.26	2/26
Tues. 27					4001.26	
Wed. 28					4001.26	
Thurs. 3/1/73	2000.26	2000.01	2000.01	2000.26	4001.01	3/1
Fri. 2						
Sat. 3						
Sun. 4						
Mon. 5						
Tues. 6						

YES, YOU CAN
be secure, happy, and rich

Throughout this book I've stressed the importance of building a nest egg, of having an umbrella when the rains come. But the pursuit of wealth is in itself not, and seldom has been, the pursuit of happiness. To become rich is not an end in itself. It is a means to an end. I didn't always know this. I had to find it out. The hard way.

Penniless and fresh out of college at the age of nineteen, I went to work for the U.S. Army Ordnance Department. That was just before the outbreak of the Second World War.

During the war I left government service to form an engineering company with two partners. I felt I could do more for the war effort that way. The company enjoyed immediate success. By the end of the war, we employed over 150 professional people.

When the war came to an end, there was a mad scramble by companies all over the nation to keep government contracts and to get new ones. Relations with government buying agencies were handled in many cases by sales representatives in Washington, who attempted to bring in business with shady deals. My partner who managed sales was described by one of his friends as "a man who sleeps in a bed with angles." Naturally, our sales representatives wanted to work some questionable deals of their own, and my partners went along with them.

I refused to have anything to do with their schemes.

I went on a short winter vacation. When I came back, I found I had been voted out of the business. The shock was almost unbearable. I had gone from poverty to riches in a few short years, and now the bubble had burst.

Fortunately, through that short period of success I had lived modestly and managed to build a small nest egg. I could start all over again. But first I needed to get away from it all for a while. Some of our employees who had been on a job for us in Mexico had come back with stories of orchids growing in wild profusion. Why not go to Mexico to get away from it all and at the same time look into the story of the orchids? Orchids might very well be my new business.

I spent the better part of the next two years in Mexico, growing orchids commercially and distributing them through parts of the United States. I also did research on orchids, thanks to facilities made available to me by the Rockefeller Foundation.

During my stay in Mexico I learned one of the important lessons of my life. The Mexican natives lived in abject poverty. It was a struggle for them just to stay alive. Yet, they really had much more than most of us had. They had their music, their religion, and their love of children. It was these three wonderful things that made all their privations endurable and their lives meaningful. Before my visit to Mexico and since then, I have watched people caught up in the pursuit of riches for riches' sake. But among these people I have seldom, if ever, found the fulfillment that the Mexican peasants had achieved.

The disaster that struck me when I was thrown out of a business I had helped to found and build had brought me to Mexico. It had brought me to an understanding that there's more in life than just trying to get rich. Since then I have pursued riches, but I've enjoyed life while I've been doing it. And I know the estate I've accumulated, which is still growing, makes the enjoyment of life so much more exciting. If I were to be asked the question, "Why do you pursue riches?" I would say, "To enjoy life. And the only way to enjoy life is—first—*to be secure.*"

Today I am secure enough that, no matter what life may hold in the future, I'll be able to weather any financial storm and my family will always be provided for. Just knowing *that* is a source of great enjoyment.

I hope that this book has helped show you the way to the same security. The MONEY KEYS are your basic tools. When you use them, remember that banks frequently change their rules without giving adequate notice. The bank rules on which the MONEY KEYS are based may be changed in this fashion at some future date. What you have to do is keep abreast of the changes. The changes may force some variations in some of the *Keys.* Make those changes yourself. By working with the *Keys* in this book you've gained an invaluable insight into how to use bank rules to get the most for your savings dollar.

As you continue in the years ahead to get more out of your income while living well within your means, you will create a still better life and a more secure future for yourself and your loved ones.

And if you'll take pride in whatever you do and create a better product or provide a better service, you will make this country not only a better place for your fellow men but also a better place for yourself and your family.

But, remember, none of this is possible without putting your hands on found money—and saving it.

YES, YOU *CAN* get out of debt.

YES, YOU *CAN* stay out of debt.

YES, YOU *CAN* live better.

YES, YOU *CAN* build an estate.

YES, YOU *CAN* make this country and this world a better place to live in.

Can you be secure, happy, and rich?

YES, YOU *CAN!*

BONUS

Seven *FOUND* MONEY KEYS
to start you from scratch
to an estate in excess of
a quarter of a million dollars

FOUND Money Key No. 1

Pick up $200 a year
operating your car

In most areas of the country, there are self-service gasoline stations. By serving yourself, you can usually save time—and money too: 3 cents, 4 cents, 5 cents, and, in some cases, 6 cents a gallon. Since most of us buy more than 1,000 gallons of gasoline a year, savings up to $60 a year are possible for a one-car family. You can't always get a 6-cent discount, so figure on a saving of about $50 a year.

Across the country, even in the big cities, the motorist comes across off brands of gasoline; not Esso, Mobil, Texaco, or Gulf, but brand names that aren't as familiar. Many of these brands are sold by chains; not by chains of, say, a hundred thousand stations but by chains of perhaps a hundred.

Many people are afraid they'll damage their cars by buying these gasolines; and I'll grant that, all other things equal, I too would pull up to the name-brand pumps. But that's why all other things are *not* equal. In order to compete, these off-brand gasolines have to offer some incentives; they're 2, 3, 4, or 5 cents per gallon cheaper than name-brand gasolines.

Is your car damaged when you use off-brand gasolines? The unanimous answer I've received all over the country is:

"The only difference is the price."

Use off-brand gasolines and you can save about $50 a year.

Off-brand gasolines are frequently found in self-service stations. That means a double saving. On a recent trip, I was able to cut gas costs as much as 10 cents a gallon by driving into self-service stations offering off brands. I had no difficulty finding stations of this kind all over the country.

Fill up your tank with off-brand gas at self-service stations —and save about $100 a year.

If your engine doesn't ping or knock when you're accelerating sharply, *it doesn't need high-test gasoline.* (Hint: If your engine does ping or knock, a simple tune-up will set it right.) Even Sun Oil flatly states that 80 to 90% of car owners using high-test or premium gasoline can do just as well with regular gasoline. By switching to regular gasoline, you can save yourself about $50 per year.

Recommended tire pressures are fine for local low-speed driving. But for modern highway speeds, some automobile manufacturers advise you to increase your tire pressure. It would be a good idea to check with your car manual or dealer to find out how much of an increase is advisable. Here's a rule of thumb: For high speeds, increase front-wheel pressure 10%, rear-wheel pressure 15%.

Increasing tire pressure for high-speed driving can increase the life of your tires. Tires that last two years with standard pressures can last *four* years with increased pressures. That means a considerable dollar savings. How much? Here's how I figure it:

Say a set of tires costs $200. If the tires last two years, they cost $100 a year ($200 divided by 2). If they last four years, they cost only $50 a year ($200 divided by 4). Keep the pressure up and you save $50 a year ($100 minus $50 equals $50).

Put all four ways of savings together—the use of self-service stations, off-brand gasoline, regular rather than high-test gasoline, and increased tire pressure—and you can save up to about $200 a year operating your car. Without half trying, you can certainly save half that amount. That's $100. And that's found money. Add it to your estate.

FOUND MONEY SCOREBOARD

Found Money Key	Yearly Savings
No. 1	$100 to $200
No. 2	
No. 3	
No. 4	
No. 5	
No. 6	
No. 7	
WATCH YOUR ESTATE GROW IN ONE YEAR	$100 to $200

FOUND Money Key No. 2

Gain $200 a year from car "extras"
—and ride more safely

Many extras on your car are either worthless or downright dangerous. Here are some examples:

• Power windows. In some kinds of accidents, they can fail; you can be trapped.

• Power seats. These may be a convenience, but they're not necessary. All too often they go out of order; you can't adjust your seat, and that means you can't drive safely.

• Radial tires. Radial tires are not always a desirable safety feature. According to *Consumer Reports*, some cars react poorly to this type of tire.

• Tinted glass. This does cut out some of the overhead glare, and that's fine. But at night, tinted glass cuts down visibility. That's not so fine.

• Car stereo. Seriously, how much of a stereo effect can you expect in the confined area of your car? Stereo doesn't really add to your enjoyment. But it does add to your cost.

• Car clock. A clock is handy to have on your dashboard, no question. But automobile clocks are notoriously inaccurate, subject to failure and breakdown. If you have a clock that gives the wrong time, isn't it worse than no clock at all?

• Air-conditioning. This is a wonderful luxury. But ask yourself, "Do I, in my part of the country, need it for more than a few days a year? It is worth $400 to $600?" You may decide it is. But if yours is a two-car family, wouldn't you be wiser to limit your air-conditioning to just one car? (And before you decide on air-conditioning, remember: Every time you turn on that cold blast of air, you steal engine power from your drive wheels. Think about it.)

• Power brakes and power steering. These certainly have their uses, and in big cars they're highly desirable. But in compacts and subcompacts, these expensive extras are of little real value. Imagine power steering in a Volkswagen—ridiculous! (Fact is, you can't get it in a Volkswagen.)

Extras cost when you buy them and cost when you use them.

Take gasoline. The power needed to operate your extras comes from your gasoline tank. The new full-size cars loaded with extras get only 7 miles to the gallon according to Getty Oil's radio ads. You continue to pay for your extras every time you pull up to a gas pump.

Take upkeep. Did you know that the repair of a power front seat can cost $75 to $100 of your hard-earned money? The cost of your extras goes on and on in the form of recurring maintenance bills.

Eliminate extras and you eliminate these extra operating costs. You could save as much as $200 a year.

Warning: Auto dealers make the most money on option packages, so they'll try to sell you on extras. But when you try to sell them your car three years later, you'll find they'll offer you no more for your car with extras than without extras. If you trade in your car every three years, you can save about $200 a year by not buying extras in the first place.

No matter how you look at it, if you refuse to be taken in by the sales pitch for extras you don't need and which too often are a threat to your safety, you can save up to about $200 a year. Without trying to do without too many extras, you could still come away with a savings of $100. That's *more* found money. Add it to your estate.

FOUND MONEY SCOREBOARD

Found Money Key	*Yearly Savings*
No. 1	$100 to $200
No. 2	$100 to $200
No. 3	
No. 4	
No. 5	
No. 6	
No. 7	
WATCH YOUR ESTATE GROW IN ONE YEAR	$200 to $400

FOUND Money Key No. 3

Make $800 every year
when you buy a car

Buying a car? Keep in mind the cost of running it. Let me give you some rule-of-thumb operating figures for 1973:

It will cost $900 to run a subcompact car; $1,100 to run a compact car; $1,400 to run a standard-size car; and $1,700 to run a luxury car. (Figures are based on U.S. Department of Transportation statistics and estimated 1973 prices.)

Look what happens when you switch from a luxury car to a standard: Yearly operating cost goes down from $1,700 to $1,400. You make $300 a year!

When you buy a subcompact instead of a luxury car, your operating costs dip to $900 from a high of $1,700, and you make $800 a year.

In some rare cases, you can make even more. It happened in my family.

My wife was given a lovely gift by a rich uncle, a Buick Electra 220—all 4,400 pounds of it. It was wonderful for long trips on open highways, traveling at highway speeds. On those trips the Electra averaged 14 miles per gallon.

But most of the time, my wife used her car locally. On *those* trips her Electra averaged 5½ miles per gallon. Her Volkswagen station wagon (square back), that she had previously used locally, averaged 20 miles per gallon. For the Electra, gas costs figured out to 8 cents a mile; for the Volkswagen, less than 2 cents a mile. On the 10,000 miles my wife drove in a year, that difference of 6 cents a mile amounted to $600! When I added the higher cost of maintenance and repairs on the Electra to the gas costs, I found that the difference between operating an Electra and a Volkswagen for local trips came to a good $1,000 a year. (You don't have to be reminded that the original cost of the big car was about double that of the little one.)

But that $1,000 figure is unusual. The maximum saving in operating costs that you can expect by buying a smaller car is about $800. But let's say you save only half of that—$400. That's *more* found money. Add it to your estate.

FOUND MONEY SCOREBOARD

Found Money Key	Yearly Savings
No. 1	$100 to $200
No. 2	$100 to $200
No. 3	$400 to $800
No. 4	
No. 5	
No. 6	
No. 7	

WATCH YOUR
ESTATE GROW
IN ONE YEAR $600 to $1,200

FOUND Money Key No. 4

Keep your car for ten years
—and make $4,000

In the previous FOUND MONEY KEY, I told you that the standard-size car costs about $1,400 a year to run. That's based on the assumption that you'll keep the car for ten years (that's the average life of an American car). But trade in your car every three years just to be in style, and your operating cost goes up by about $250 a year. (This figure is based on the same sources used in FOUND MONEY KEY No. 3.)

Don't trade in your standard-size car every three years. Keep it for ten years. Then, even including the cost of maintenance, you'll save about $250 a year—$2,500 over ten years.

Warning: If you have a subcompact, you don't gain anything in yearly operating costs when you keep the car for ten years. But when you keep a luxury car for ten years, you save $400 a year on operating costs—$4,000 over ten years.

So when you keep your car for ten years, your savings can range from zero (subcompact) to $400 a year (luxury). Whatever you do save is found money. Add it to your estate.

FOUND MONEY SCOREBOARD

Found Money Key	Yearly Savings
No. 1	$100 to $200
No. 2	$100 to $200
No. 3	$400 to $800
No. 4	$000 to $400
No. 5	
No. 6	
No. 7	
WATCH YOUR ESTATE GROW IN ONE YEAR	$400 to $800

FOUND Money Key No. 5

Enjoy your vacation more—
while pocketing $200 in two weeks

Americans have taken to wheels for their vacations. In the summer, there are millions of people on the highways. The roads are clogged, not only with cars but with campers, trailers, and mobile homes.

If you're one of the growing number of Americans who take their vacations in the family car, here are some ways of cutting costs and having a better time. You'll come home with found money. I know it can be done because I did it.

I stopped in motels. I had accommodations for four people: my wife and me and our two children—a girl of twelve and a boy of fifteen. Our reservations called for either (1) a double bed and two single beds; (2) a double bed, a single bed, and a rollaway; or (3) a double bed and two rollaways. The price of the room was figured on the basis of three separate sleeping units: a double bed and two singles.

I found that the accommodations I reserved averaged about $27.50 per night. When you recall that during the early 1940s you could get "tourist cabins" (at that time they weren't called motels) for $1 per person per night and during the 1950s you could stay at motels rated "very good" or "excellent" for $5 or $6 per night, you realize with a shock what inflation has done to the value of your hard-earned dollar.

I found that I could beat the high cost of reserved motel rooms.

Now remember, the rooms at the motels at which I had reserved space ranged in price from about $22 to $36, for an average of about $27.50. But as I passed through the areas in which I was vacationing, I saw signs on other motels advertising lower rates. Here's a typical sign: "Singles $6, Doubles $8 —$1 per extra person." I could have stayed in one of these motels with my family for only $10.

I decided to try them. I found that the rooms at these independent motels were just as pleasant, just as clean, just as modern as those at the more expensive chain motels at which I had reserved space. In some cases the facilities were even better. And my family and I always got more personal attention. Prices averaged $10 to $14 a night. What a savings compared to $22 to $36!

You'll find it hard to reserve space in these independent motels because they're seldom listed in the guidebooks, they're not well advertised, and if you use a travel agent, he probably never heard of them. If you insist on reservations, you'll have to go to the well-advertised chain motels listed in the guidebooks and pay the much higher prices. But I found you can have a carefree vacation *without* making reservations.

You can be reasonably sure of finding the accommodations you need in independent motels if you just follow this advice:

Plan your vacation so you're on the road early—get up, say, at about 6 A.M. Call it a day around 4 P.M., and keep your eyes open for a nice-looking independently owned motel. Watch for the signs: "Rooms—$6 and up." Stop at a few of these motels and look them over before you check in. What you look for are good, clean beds, a working air conditioner, a working radio or television set, a clean bath, and clean towels and linens. Don't feel uncomfortable when you go back to the first motel you inspected after you've given two or three other motels the once-over. At about 4 P.M., you can be pretty sure of finding the *inexpensive* motel of your choice. Settle down for an early dinner with the wonderful feeling that you're saving a lot of money.

With a family of four, you can save as much as $17.50 a day on room costs (spending $10 at an independent motel as compared to $27.50 at a chain motel). On a two-week trip, that comes to more than $200! Without half trying, you certainly can save half of that—$100. And that's *more* found money. Put it in your estate.

FOUND MONEY SCOREBOARD

Found Money Key	*Yearly Savings*
No. 1	$100 to $200
No. 2	$100 to $200
No. 3	$400 to $800
No. 4	$000 to $400
No. 5	$100 to $200
No. 6	
No. 7	
WATCH YOUR ESTATE GROW IN ONE YEAR	$700 to $1,800

FOUND Money Key No. 6

Eat better and live healthier
while getting an extra $500 a year

I'm sure you're not one of those people who go in for the current craze for "organic" foods or fall for other health-food fads. You know how much money you can waste paying puffed-up prices for food that tastes awful. You know the dangers of faddist diets; the "macrobiotic" diet actually resulted in the death of several people. But what you may not know—and what others like you who eat good, solid American food may not know— is that you can eat even better than you do and save a good deal of money while doing it. Here are just a few ways we do just that at my home:

Do you realize how much of the food you buy ends up in the garbage pail or down the drain? Not consciously wasted, but thrown away because you just don't know how much nutritional value the food contains? Reasonably authoritative sources have estimated that one-fifth of the food value of all the food we buy is wasted in this way.

For example, you throw away the outer leaves of a head of lettuce, don't you? You prefer the heart. But the outer leaves of most green vegetables are far more nutritious than the tastier inner leaves. The outer leaves should never be discarded. Why throw away a large percentage of the value you pay good money for?

Now I'll grant that the outer leaves of a vegetable don't taste quite as good as the inner leaves, but there are ways of making them taste as good or better. At our house we mix those otherwise wasted leaves into a salad. A mixed salad of the outer leaves of lettuce, turnips, broccoli, collard greens, kale, and so on, with a homemade salad dressing of oil, vinegar, and spices, is delicious—and packed with food value. Sometimes, we take those outer leaves and boil them up into a soup that's a favorite of every member of my family.

Or take potatoes. Did you know that the best part of the potato—the part with the most vitamins—is directly underneath the skin? Yet most people cut away the part of the potato directly under the skin when they peel a potato before cooking it. At our house we bake or boil our potatoes in their jackets. Try it and you'll be in for a taste treat. The skin of a baked potato tastes just as good or better than the inside.

The way most of us cook vegetables is wasteful too. Do you throw away the most valuable part of the vegetable—the water it's cooked in? The chances are you do. "Why shouldn't I continue to throw it away?" you ask. "Even if the water is good for me and my family, it tastes dreadful."

But it needn't taste dreadful. In our kitchen, we cook our vegetables, seasoned to taste, in a tightly covered pan with a minimum, minimum, minimum amount of water—just enough to prevent scorching. The vegetables come out tender and delicious that way—crunchy, not mushy. But it's the small amount of liquid that's the real prize. It's full of nutrition and real tasty. Instead of pouring it down the drain, put it in a jar, store it in the refrigerator, and use it the next time you make soup.

Of course, I'm talking about fresh vegetables. So many of us have become addicted to eating frozen and canned vegetables that we no longer remember what a fresh vegetable tastes like. Fresh vegetables taste good and are good for you—not only nutritionally but financially. Switch to fresh vegetables, and you'll notice how much further your food dollar goes.

Now that you know some of the ways my family avoids wasting that one-fifth of the food value that most of us throw away, I'm sure you can think of other ways of avoiding waste' in your own kitchen. It's important that you do so if you're bent on building your estate. When you stop slopping good food into the garbage, you not only eat better and live healthier because of improved nutrition but *you also get more edible food for your money.*

Or look at it this way: Because you're throwing away a much smaller percentage of your food, you buy less food—and that saves you money. How much money? Figure that the average family of four spends about $2,500 per year for food. If that family does not waste one-fifth (20%) of real food value, it can save $500 a year (20% of $2,500). Without half trying, you should be able to come out of the kitchen ahead by at least about $250 this year. And that's found money. Add it to your estate.

FOUND MONEY SCOREBOARD

Found Money Key	*Yearly Savings*
No. 1	$100 to $200
No. 2	$100 to $200
No. 3	$400 to $800
No. 4	$000 to $400
No. 5	$100 to $200
No. 6	$250 to $500
No. 7	

IN ONE YEAR
WATCH YOUR $950 to $2,300
ESTATE GROW

FOUND Money Key No. 7

Learn one new word—
and pocket $200 a year

Medicines—they're expensive. But not if you learn one new word—*generic*. When you use the generic names of the medicines you need, you can save solid sums of money.

Let me give you an example to show you what I mean by a generic name. You've heard of penicillin. But have you ever heard of Compicillin-VK? Compicillin-VK is a *brand* name of a type of penicillin. There are many brand names of that type of penicillin. "Penicillin" is the *generic* name.

Another example. You're familiar with cortisone. You're not familiar, are you, with Cortef or Cortril? Cortef is a brand of cortisone manufactured by the Upjohn Company, and Cortril is Pfizer's cortisone. There are many brand names for cortisone. "Cortisone" is the generic name.

At one time or another, a doctor may have prescribed the antibiotic Achromycin for you or your family. "Achromycin" is Lederle's brand name for the antibiotic with the generic name "tetracycline."

I'd like to tell you a story about Achromycin and tetracycline.

The night before my mother-in-law, who is in her late seventies, was to return to her home in Florida, she seemed to be concerned about a congestion in her chest. Our family doctor came over, examined her, and prescribed four 250-milligram tablets of tetracycline a day for five days, a total of 20 tablets.

I ordinarily keep a stock of tetracycline in our house for the simple reason that it's a broad-spectrum antibiotic that both my doctor and the children's pediatrician have constantly prescribed. I had become accustomed to buying tetracycline in quantities of 100 capsules for $1.20 to $1.30. That's about 1¼ cents per capsule.

When I went to the medicine chest, I discovered that I had only eight tablets left. My mother-in-law was leaving around noon the following day, so the doctor gave her a revised prescription for 12 tablets of tetracycline. The following morning, my wife went to a local pharmacy. She simply handed over the prescription, and the pharmacist filled it with *Achromycin*. The twelve capsules cost $2.35—just about 20 cents a capsule. And I had been buying the same product under its generic name, tetracycline, for only 1¼ cents per capsule!

YES, YOU *CAN* buy your medicines much, much cheaper when you *order by generic name, not by brand name.* One wholesale drug distributor claims that when you "buy by generic name [you] save up to 90% of [the] cost of comparable national brand products."

You can also save on vitamins in this way. Several pharmaceutical firms now specialize in exactly duplicating national-brand vitamin formulas. The catalogs of these firms (get them by mail or at some local pharmacies) supply you with comparison charts. You'll have no difficulty finding equivalents of the big-brand vitamins at one-quarter to one-half the price.

How do you get to know the generic name of drugs? When your doctor writes a prescription, ask him if a generic-name drug is just as good as a brand name. If he says yes, ask him to write the generic name, not a brand name, on the prescription.

Make sure that, when you present the prescription to your pharmacist, you don't simply hand it over as my wife did. Say to the pharmacist, "I want this prescription filled with the least expensive generic drug—not with a brand-name drug."

Make use of generic names of medicines and you'll find, as I have, that you'll have no trouble saving money. How much money? I've saved as much as two-thirds of the cost of brand-name products. A family of four, according to Internal Revenue Service experts I've spoken to, spends about $300 a year on medicines. Two-thirds of $300 is $200. You can easily save half of that $300, or $150. (Even if your family is one of the fortunate ones that spends only $150 a year on medicines, you can still save $100.) That's *still more* found money. Add it to your estate.

FOUND MONEY SCOREBOARD

Found Money Key	Yearly Savings
No. 1	$100 to $200
No. 2	$100 to $200
No. 3	$400 to $800
No. 4	$000 to $400
No. 5	$100 to $200
No. 6	$250 to $500
No. 7	$150 to $200
WATCH YOUR ESTATE GROW IN ONE YEAR	$1,100 to $2,500

Build an estate of a quarter million dollars in thirty years— starting from scratch

Using just the previous seven *FOUND* MONEY KEYS, and starting with nothing in the bank, you can add between $1,100 and $2,500 to your estate every year.

Here's what happens when you invest that found money each year at the maximum advertised rate for savings certificates, 6% (effective yield as high as 6.27%):

WATCH YOUR
ESTATE GROW
(before taxes)

End of first year	$1,100	to	$2,500
End of tenth year	$15,000	to	$33,000
End of twentieth year	$42,000	to	$94,000
End of thirtieth year	$91,000	to	$206,000

But when you use the other MONEY KEYS in this book, without half trying you can invest your found money safely at an effective yield of about 8%, with these happier results:

WATCH YOUR
ESTATE GROW
(before taxes)

End of first year	$1,100	to	$2,500
End of tenth year	$16,000	to	$36,000
End of twentieth year	$50,000	to	$115,000
End of thirtieth year	$125,000	to	$283,000

Examine those figures. Let me repeat what I told you in the first section of this book: "Most of the guidelines will make more and more money for you. If you waste that money, you will never be any richer than you are today. But add that money to your estate, and you will not only be richer in dollars but also in the sense of having achieved a goal that is unattainable to the vast majority of people." Remember that your estate can start from nothing—provided you're willing to forego fashionable, meaningless luxuries. Now answer this question:

Which would you prefer: Cadillacs now and retirement on social security, or Volkswagens now and a quarter-million-dollar estate in thirty years?

The choice is yours.